Britain and the American Revolution

ELIZABETH WARDLE

CYCLOPS (Mike M)

Hodder & Stoughton
LONDON SYDNEY AUCKLAND

ACKNOWLEDGEMENTS

The Publishers would like to thank the following for permission to reproduce illustrations in this volume:

Peter Newark's American Pictures – cover.
The Bettman Archive – contents.
Colonial Williamsburg Foundation p. 6 both.
The Bettman Archive p. 7 top.
Peter Newark's American Pictures p. 7 lower.
William Sidney Mount: 'Cider Making', The Metropolitan Museum of Art p. 9 left.
The New York Historical Society p. 9 right.
National Gallery of Art, Andrew C. Mellon Collection p. 11 lower left.
Abby Aldrich Rockefeller Folk Art Center p. 11 top.
The Bettman Archive p. 12 right.
Peter Newark's American Pictures p. 14 both.
The Historical Society of Pennsylvania p. 16 top.
The J. Allan Cash Photolibrary p. 17 top.
Gift of the Artist's Great-Grandaughter, Courtesy Museum of Fine Arts, Boston p. 18.
The American Museum in Britain, Claverton Manor p. 19 top.
United States Travel & Tourism/Audience Planners p. 19 lower.
Courtesy of the John Carter Brown Library at Brown University p. 20.
Peter Newark's American Pictures p. 21 top.
'The Sargent Family' Gift of Edgar William and Bernice Chrysler Garbisch © 1993.
National Gallery of Art, Washington p. 22 left.
Courtesy of the Maryland Historical Society, Baltimore p. 22 right.
Massachusetts Historical Society p. 23.
Courtesy of the Bostonian Society, Old State House p. 24.
Peter Newark's American Pictures p. 25; p. 27.
Courtesy of the Bostonian Society, Old State House p. 28.
Peter Newark's American Pictures p. 29.
Courtesy of the Bostonian Society, Old State House p. 30.
Courtesy of the American Antiquarian Society p. 31.
Peter Newark's American Pictures p. 32 lower.
Gift of Joseph W. William and Edward H.R. Revere Courtesy, Museum of Fine Arts, Boston p. 32 top.
Mr and Mrs J. William Middendorf II Collection p. 32 lower.
Peter Newark's American Pictures p. 36; p. 37; p. 39.
The Library of Congress p. 40 left.
The J. Allan Cash Photolibrary p. 40 right.
Peter Newark's American Pictures p. 41.
UPI/Bettman p. 42.
The New York Public Library p. 44.
The British Museum p. 46.
Peter Newark's American Pictures p. 48.
Munson-Williams-Proctor Institute, Museum of Art, Utica, New York p. 49 top.
Wadsworth Atheneum, Hartford, Connecticut, Purchased by Subscription p. 49 lower.
The National Portrait Gallery, London p. 51.
The New York Public Library p. 52.
The Bettman Archive p. 53.
Lauros-Giraudon p. 54.
Musée de la Ville de Paris, Musée Carnavalet/Giraudon p. 55 left; p. 55 right.
British Museum/Michael Holford p. 56.
Peter Newark's American Pictures p. 57.
Manchester Public Libraries p. 58–59.
The British Museum p. 59.
Lawrence Impey Collection p. 60.
The J. Allen Cash Photolibrary p. 61.
United States Travel & Tourism Administration p. 62 left.
Peter Newark's American Pictures p. 63 left.
Colonial Williamsburg Foundation p. 63 right.

Every effort has been made to trace and acknowledge ownership of copyright. The Publishers will be glad to make suitable arrangements with any copyright holders whom it has not been possible to contact.

Illustrations by Gay Galsworthy

For my mother and her friends at Waterton House

British Library Cataloguing in Publication Data
Wardle, Elizabeth
Britain and the American Revolution. –
(Past Historic Series)
I. Title II. Series
973.3

ISBN 0 340 52307 7

First published 1993
Impression number 10 9 8 7 6 5 4 3 2 1
Year 1988 1997 1996 1995 1994 1993

Typeset by Litho Link Ltd, Welshpool, Powys, Wales.
Printed for the educational publishing division of Hodder and Stoughton Ltd, Mill Road, Dunton Green, Sevenoaks, Kent by Colorcraft Ltd, Hong Kong.

CONTENTS

SEAL OF THE PRESIDENT OF THE UNITED STATES
E PLURIBUS UNUM

1 A NEW WORLD

1495 | 1550 | 1600 | 1650 | 1700 | 1750 | 1800

The USA stretches over thousands of miles from the Atlantic to the Pacific Ocean, and from Mexico up to the Canadian border. It is the most powerful country in the western world.

However, if you had crossed the Atlantic in 1750 you wouldn't have found the USA. Depending on where you went, you would have met settlers and explorers from different European countries. Many were British, and they lived in 13 settlements stretching down the Atlantic Coast. You can see these settlements in source A. They were called colonies, and the people who lived in them were colonists.

The biggest area of North America was lived in only by the American Indians, who had been there for thousands of years.

A Explorers and settlers in eastern America. The shaded area on the small map is the area covered by the 13 colonies on the main map.

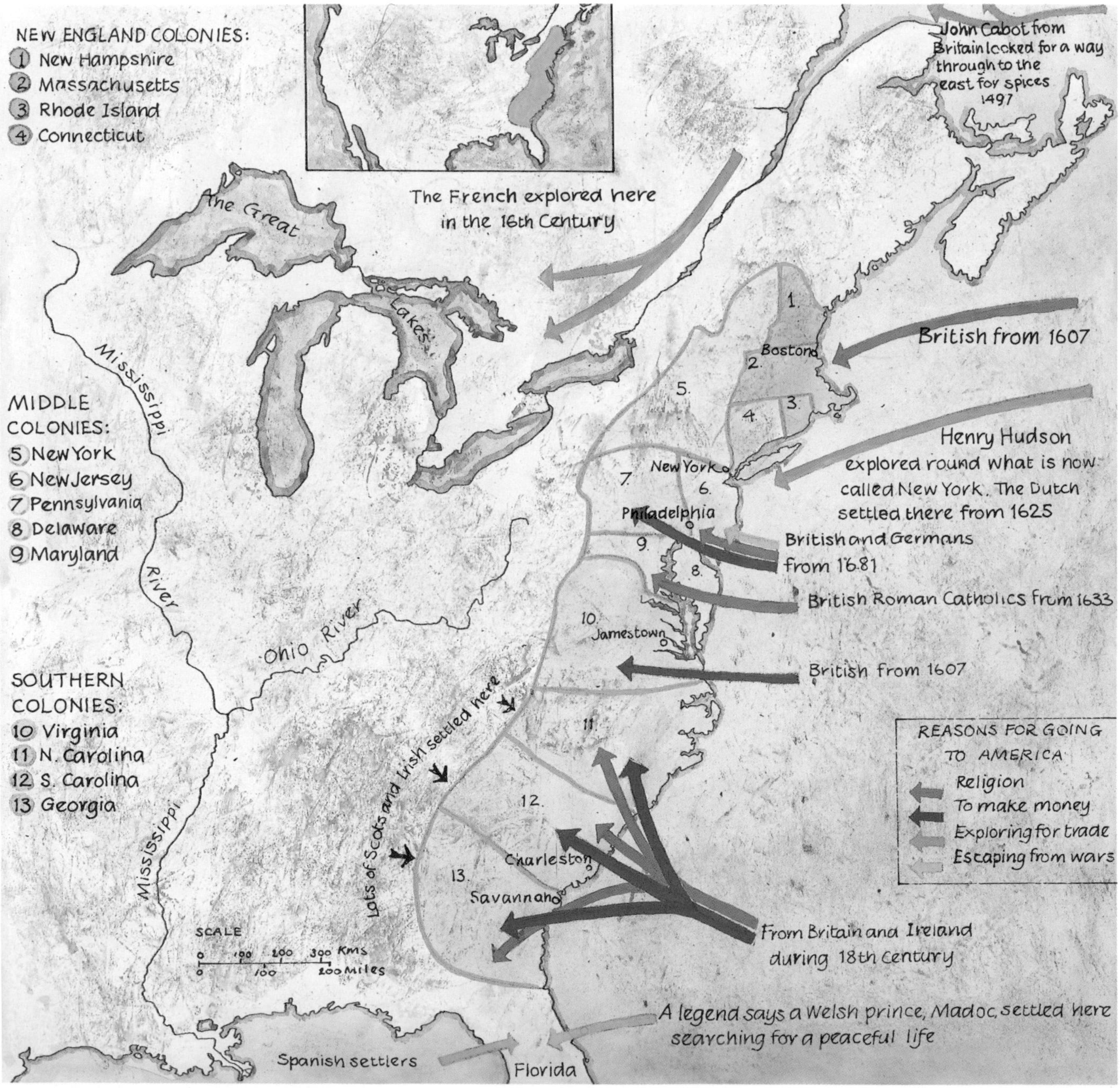

NEW ENGLAND COLONIES:
1 New Hampshire
2 Massachusetts
3 Rhode Island
4 Connecticut
MIDDLE COLONIES:
5 New York
6 New Jersey
7 Pennsylvania
8 Delaware
9 Maryland
SOUTHERN COLONIES:
10 Virginia
11 N. Carolina
12 S. Carolina
13 Georgia
John Cabot from Britain looked for a way through to the east for spices 1497
The French explored here in the 16th Century
The Great Lakes
Mississippi River
Ohio River
British from 1607
Boston
New York
Philadelphia
Jamestown
Charleston
Savannah
Henry Hudson explored round what is now called New York. The Dutch settled there from 1625
British and Germans from 1681
British Roman Catholics from 1633
British from 1607
Lots of Scots and Irish settled here
REASONS FOR GOING TO AMERICA
Religion
To make money
Exploring for trade
Escaping from wars
From Britain and Ireland during 18th Century
SCALE
0 100 200 300 Kms
0 100 200 Miles
A legend says a Welsh prince, Madoc, settled here searching for a peaceful life
Spanish settlers
Florida

Would-be settlers were prepared to risk the dangerous, uncomfortable voyage for many different reasons. They were a very mixed bunch. Some were the sons of wealthy lords. Some were so poor that they had to sell themselves to an employer for several years in order to pay their fares.

They belonged to many different religions. Some spoke different languages. Many were escaping from the terrible wars which had been raging across Europe for more than 100 years.

However, those who survived the journey and the first few years did have one thing in common – they were very skilled and tough. They weren't easy people to push around.

C Captain Seagull, in a comic play called *Eastward Hoe* (1605), described all the wealth of Virginia.

> All their pans and their chamber pots are pure gold. All the prisoners they take are [chained] in gold. And for rubies and diamonds, they go forth on holidays and gather 'em by the seashore to hang on their children's coats.

Historians have to study their sources very carefully. For example, source C is an extract from a play. It pokes fun at people who went to Virginia hoping to make their fortunes without doing any work. Even though it was written as a joke, historians have to decide whether this source is useful – in other words, whether it tells them anything.

1 a) Look at source A. Roughly calculate how many miles it is from New Hampshire to the south of Georgia.
b) List the problems which you think modern Americans may have to face because of the size of their country.
c) Make a list of the advantages there must be in living in such a large country.

2 Work with a partner.
a) Read source C. Do you think Captain Seagull was telling the truth about what could be found in Virginia? Give reasons.
b) How might this source be useful to you if you were trying to work out reasons why people went to America?
c) Study source A. How many reasons can you find why people went to America? Write them down.
d) List all the sources in the chapter which help you to understand why people made this difficult journey. Now, draw a diagram which shows as many of the reasons as possible.

Life in Europe between 1618 and 1763 must have seemed like one long war. Ordinary people suffered BECAUSE
They might get forced to join the army or navy.
Their taxes rose to pay for the wars.
Their crops were ruined or stolen by passing armies.
New rulers often made them change their religion.

B Life in Europe between 1618 and 1763 must have seemed like one long war.

2 HOW THE COLONIES WERE GOVERNED

Nearly everyone who settled in the 13 British colonies had gone there to become more independent. Because the colonies were such a long way from Britain this was normally quite easy.

Each colony had a Governor, who looked after the colony on behalf of King George III. He had a Council to advise him. This was chosen from the leading men of the colony. There was also an elected Assembly (a local Parliament). This decided on laws and taxes. Each colony had a constitution – a set of rules for government.

A Anthony Stokes, an Englishman, writing in 1783, described how most colonial governments worked.

The charters of these colonies, gave the people power to elect all their Officers except those of the Admiralty and Customs.

The General Assemblies in the Colonies, together with their Council [and the King's] Governor, make laws suited to their own emergencies [as long as these are] agreeable to the laws of Great Britain.

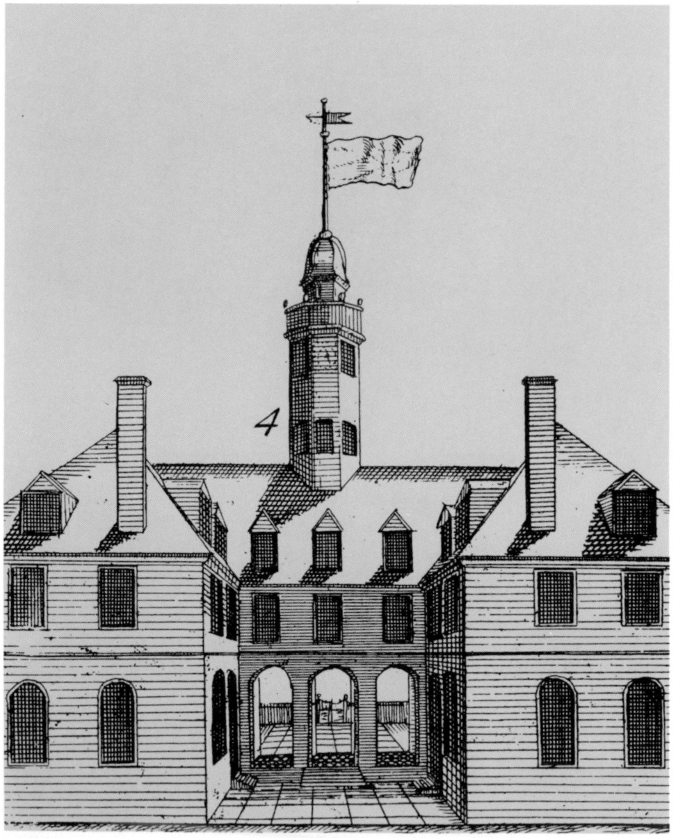
4

B The Virginia Capitol (Parliament House), completed at Williamsburg, 1705.

C Inside the Virginia Capitol. (This is a reconstruction of the original building.) This picture shows where the representatives sat. The Speaker's chair is in the middle.

1 Look at sources B and C.

a) From the following words and phrases choose the six which you think best describe the Virginia Capitol and write them down:
crowded, lots of space, well-lit, dark, panelled walls, peeling walls, well-furnished, badly furnished, carefully-laid flooring, dirt flooring, nicely designed and well-built, ugly and badly-built.

b) Do you think the Virginians were proud that they had their own Parliament? Give reasons for your answer.

At least one man in four could vote for the colonial assemblies, as long as he was a freeman, not a slave. In Britain only one man in 30 had the right to vote. Women could not vote in Britain or America.

D Pilgrims on the *Mayflower* working out a plan for ruling their new colony in 1620. They had sailed to America so that they could worship God and live in their own way.

It is sometimes difficult to understand why characters in history acted or thought as they did. To try to understand, we usually need to combine three things: a study of the available sources, our knowledge of history, and our own common sense.

2 Look at source D.
a) What are the women doing?
b) Why are they not taking part in the decision-making?
c) How do you think the women would feel about this?
d) How do you think the men would feel about it?
e) What do *you* feel about it? Give reasons.

Some towns, such as Boston, had regular town meetings. Every man with land valued at £20 could vote. They chose the Boston representatives for the Massachusetts Colonial Assembly, and 200 other unpaid officials to run the town. They often annoyed the Massachusetts Governor.

E Governor Shirley complained about the Boston Town Meetings in the middle of the 18th century:

The [main] cause of the mobbish turn in this town is in its constitution. [It is run by] the population in their town meetings where the [lowest inhabitants] . . . by their constant attendance outvote all the gentlemen merchants, [important] traders and all the better [class] of inhabitants.

F Faneuil Hall, built in 1742 specially for the Boston Town Meetings.

3 Read source E.
a) What sort of people does Governor Shirley mean when he speaks of the 'lowest inhabitants'?
b) Whom does he think should have the most say in the Town Meetings?
c) Why do you suppose he thinks like this?
d) If you could talk to some of the 'lowest inhabitants' of Boston, what might *they* say about their right to take part in the Town Meetings?

4 You are a citizen of Boston. Explain to a newcomer from Britain how your local system of government works, or, if you prefer, draw them a diagram to explain it.

3 WORKING IN THE COLONIES

There were lots of different ways of earning a living in the colonies, but they all involved hard work. The sea played a large part in many people's lives. They either built boats, or fished from them, or used them to carry a vast range of goods to and from America.

About 100 years earlier, Parliament in London had passed laws to control trade with the colonies. These laws are known as the Navigation Acts. The idea was that the mother country and the colonies should produce everything that they needed. Nothing should be bought from outside.

The colonies were supposed to send their products (see source A) just to Britain or to British colonies, and only in British or colonial ships. Britain was to provide the colonies with all the manufactured goods they needed.

This system gave the colonies a guaranteed market for their produce. They could earn a good

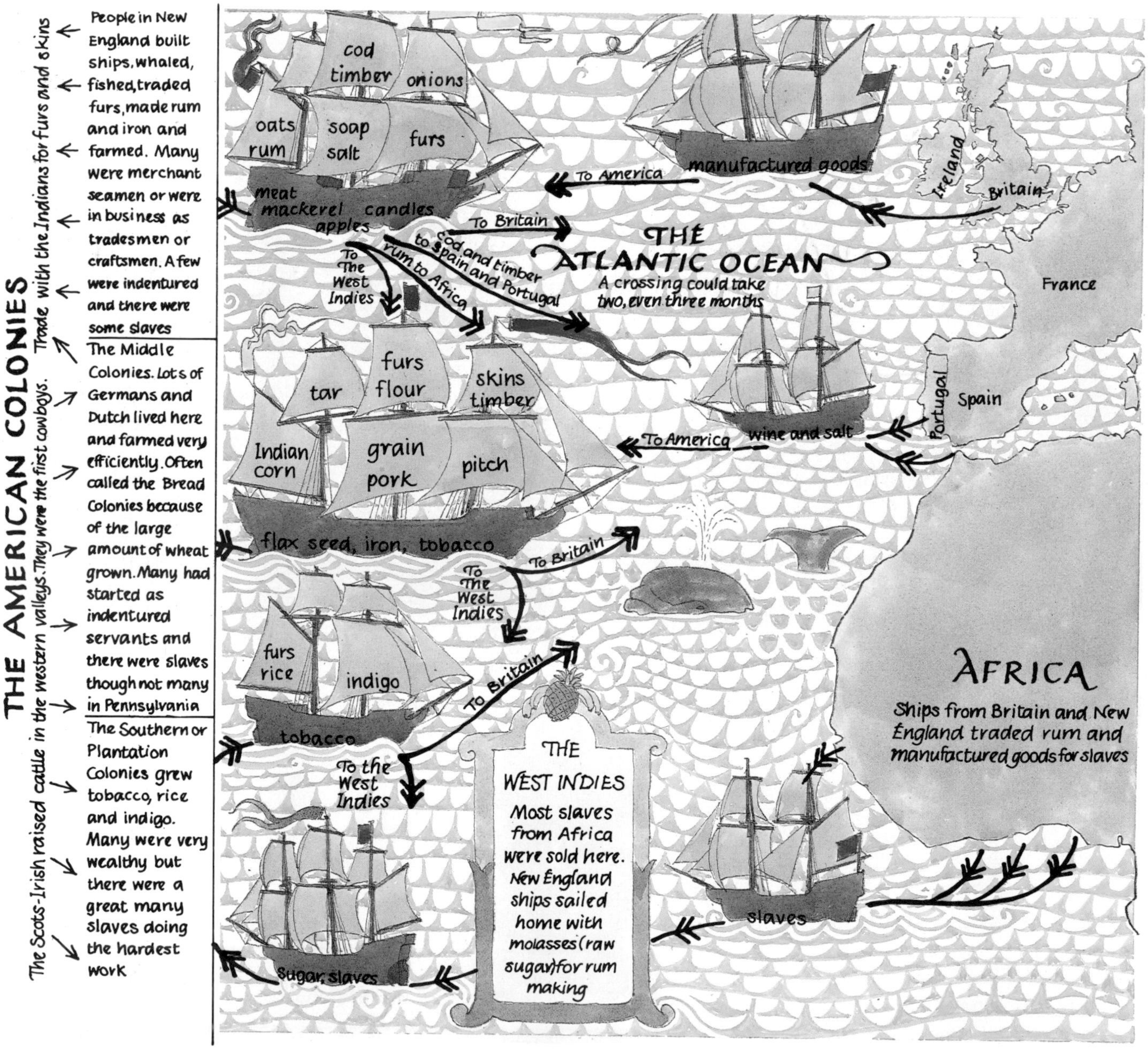

THE AMERICAN COLONIES
Trade with the Indians for furs and skins
The Scots-Irish raised cattle in the western valleys. They were the first cowboys.
People in New England built ships, whaled, fished, traded furs, made rum and iron and farmed. Many were merchant seamen or were in business as tradesmen or craftsmen. A few were indentured and there were some slaves
The Middle Colonies. Lots of Germans and Dutch lived here and farmed very efficiently. Often called the Bread Colonies because of the large amount of wheat grown. Many had started as indentured servants and there were slaves though not many in Pennsylvania
The Southern or Plantation Colonies grew tobacco, rice and indigo. Many were very wealthy but there were a great many slaves doing the hardest work
cod
timber
onions
oats
rum
soap
salt
furs
meat
mackerel
candles
apples
manufactured goods
To America
Ireland
Britain
To Britain
THE ATLANTIC OCEAN
A crossing could take two, even three months
To The West Indies
cod and timber to Spain and Portugal
rum to Africa
France
furs
flour
tar
skins
timber
Indian corn
grain
pork
pitch
flax seed, iron, tobacco
To America
wine and salt
Portugal
Spain
To Britain
To The West Indies
furs
rice
indigo
tobacco
To Britain
To the West Indies
AFRICA
Ships from Britain and New England traded rum and manufactured goods for slaves
THE WEST INDIES
Most slaves from Africa were sold here. New England ships sailed home with molasses (raw sugar) for rum making
slaves
sugar, slaves

A Colonial trade and production.

living, and their shipping was always protected by the British navy.

This was very useful indeed in the first part of the 18th century, when Britain and France were often at war. However, after these wars ended in 1763 the colonists felt much safer. They now wanted to decide for themselves how to trade, and who to trade with. There was a great deal of smuggling.

Historians need to notice how things change during the period they are studying. Sometimes changes happen gradually. Sometimes one event makes things change quickly.

1 a) Why would the Navigation Acts be good for Britain?
b) Look at source A. Make a list of the kinds of manufactured goods which you think Britain exported to the colonies.
c) What benefits did the colonists get from the Navigation Acts?
d) Which event in 1763 changed the colonists' attitude to the Acts?
e) What do you think colonial merchants would say if you, a person from Britain, told them that smuggling was against the law?

B Many colonists ran farms. In this picture you can see a busy northern farm, where cider is being made.

Craftswomen and men were much in demand all over the colonies. The town of Lancaster, in Pennsylvania, became famous for rifles, covered wagons, and all kinds of leather goods. Most boys were apprenticed to some craft or trade, but only a few girls were.

One young Boston man, Benjamin Franklin, found the place too quiet. He ran away to Philadelphia and became an apprentice printer. In source C you can see him at work in his own printing shop which he opened in 1728. In time, he had his own newspaper, and was put in charge of the colonies' new postal system.

He was destined to become even more famous for other reasons.

C Benjamin Franklin in his printing shop in 1728.

Apprentices were treated strictly. Fortunately, not many employers were like Mr and Mrs Weekes of New Hampshire. They cut off their apprentice's toes because he was lazy!

2 Look at source C.
a) Which do you suppose is Franklin and which is the customer?
b) What sort of things might the customer want to have printed?

WORK IN THE SOUTH

Life was easier for the plantation farmers of the south. Many of them used slaves or indentured servants to grow their tobacco and rice. Indentured servants often worked as hard as slaves, but at least in time they became free men and women.

A An agreement to work for an employer in America in return for money for the fare.

21st February 1682. Rich. Browne aged 33 years . . . doth promise . . . to . . . Francis Richardson for the term of foure years to serve in such service & imployment as the said Francis Richardson shall imploy him.

Francis Richardson doth [promise] to pay for his passing, and to find and allow him meat, drink, [clothing], and lodging.

Eliza Lucas lived on her father's South Carolina plantation. She was very interested in plants and she developed a valuable new crop – indigo. The indigo plant supplied the blue dye for uniforms.

The new crop brought great wealth to South Carolina. Eliza Lucas became very well respected. When she died, George Washington (the first President of the USA), asked to be one of the men who carried her coffin into church.

Getting the dye from the indigo plant was a hard, hot, slimy process. The planters thought slaves were ideal for the job, so the slave trade increased.

There were already many slaves in the colonies. They had been brought, against their will, from Africa. They had no rights and were treated like pieces of property. Some Americans objected to this. Others made so much money from slavery that it would be a long time before it was stopped.

B Different ways of using tobacco. Do you think the artist approves? Many slaves worked on tobacco growing.

THE DIVINE WEED

C Slaves relaxing in the 18th century.

D This advertisement for a runaway slave was printed in the *Virginia Gazette* in 1769.

Run away . . . a slave called Sandy, about 35 years of age. He is a shoemaker by trade. Whoever [brings him back] shall have [£2] reward . . . [signed] Thomas Jefferson.

E Entry in Thomas Jefferson's accounts in 1773:

Negro Sandy sold to Col. Charles Lewis [for] £100.

F 'The Skater' (1782). Other outdoor activities such as fishing and hunting were also popular.

G One person wrote about slaves on a plantation:

Their work is done by one or two o'clock in the afternoon, and [they] have the rest of the day to themselves, which they spend working in their own private fields . . . allowed them by their masters, for planting of rice, corn, potatoes, tobacco &c for their own use and profit.

Historians are interested in the consequences (effects) of people's actions. Sometimes these consequences are straightforward. But sometimes actions have effects that people didn't intend.

1 a) What would Eliza Lucas be hoping to do when she experimented with growing indigo?
b) Give one consequence of her action which she probably didn't intend.

2 a) What sort of people do you see or read about in sources C, D, E and G?
b) What sort of people can you see in source F?
c) Suggest at least three differences in their ways of life.
d) Suppose you told the people in source F that their use of slavery was wicked. What do you think they would reply?

3 a) If you had lived in the colonies what sort of job do you think you might have had? Give reasons.
b) What career do you hope to take up when you have completed your education?
c) How many of your classmates put a different answer for (a) than they put for (b)? Try to find out the reasons for the differences.

4 a) Make two lists. In list A write those things which most settlers might have in common. In list B put the many differences you might find among the settlers.
b) Do you think there was a typical settler? Give reasons.

4 EDUCATION

If we are studying things that happened over 200 years ago, we are not surprised to find that a lot has changed. However, we may also find that some things have not changed all that much.

The colonists worked hard to give their children the best possible start in life. They thought education was very important. As early as 1647 Massachusetts had an elementary school system. Harvard College was founded even earlier, in 1636.

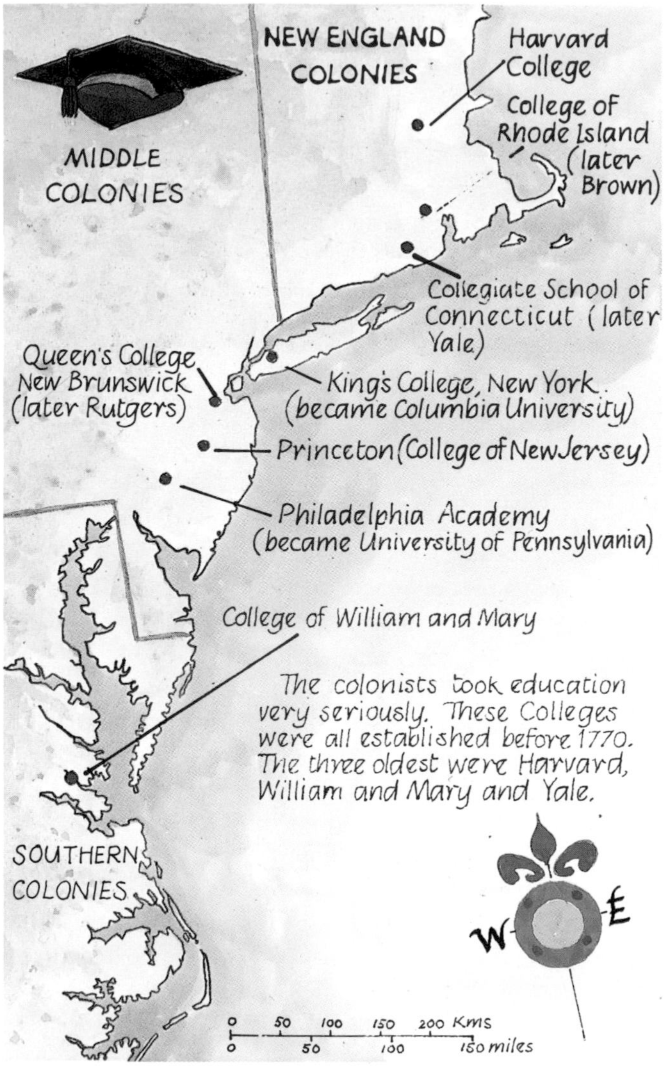

NEW ENGLAND COLONIES
MIDDLE COLONIES
SOUTHERN COLONIES
Harvard College
College of Rhode Island (later Brown)
Collegiate School of Connecticut (later Yale)
Queen's College New Brunswick (later Rutgers)
King's College, New York (became Columbia University)
Princeton (College of New Jersey)
Philadelphia Academy (became University of Pennsylvania)
College of William and Mary
The colonists took education very seriously. These Colleges were all established before 1770. The three oldest were Harvard, William and Mary and Yale.
W
E
0 50 100 150 200 Kms
0 50 100 150 miles

A Colonial colleges.

Small boys and girls would be taught to read at home, or at a 'dame' school. Only a few would get more education than that.

Most towns had a grammar school for older boys, founded by a rich citizen. Boston had five – all free, and paid for by town taxes. Even so, most boys couldn't afford to go because they had to earn a living.

Discipline at the grammar schools was very strict. Beatings were common. In winter you were expected to take wood to heat the school while you learned your Latin and Greek. If you forgot, you would shiver in the coldest corner of the room. The richest and some of the cleverest from the Boston schools might go on to Harvard College in Cambridge, just across the Charles River.

B An 18th-century colonial 'dame' school. Are all the children working hard?

C There were some schools for girls, but only for those who could pay. James Murray wrote to a relative about his daughter's boarding school in the 18th century:

You would not be pleased to see the [lazy] way in which she and the young Ladies of this place generally live. They do not get up till 8 or 9 o'clock. Breakfast is over at ten, a little reading or work until 12, dress for dinner till 2, afternoon in making or receiving visits or going about the Shops, Tea, Supper, and that closes the Day and their eyes about 11. [They probably] employ to some good purpose two hours of the twenty-four.

Slaves found it even harder than white women to get a good education, but some managed. Philadelphia and New York had free schools for teaching black children.

Many Americans who could not afford to go to grammar school continued their education at night by reading. Benjamin Franklin did this. There were at least 121 bookshops in the 13 colonies and most towns had a public library. Collections of sermons were among the most popular books.

A young man called Henry Knox opened his own bookshop and educated himself there. He specialised in military books and taught himself about military engineering. He ran his shop like a cafe – you could go for a chat, a cup of tea and a good read. Henry Knox later became one of the great generals of the Revolutionary War.

D A late 18th-century Boston bookshop, redrawn by a modern artist.

1 Copy this grid into your exercise book and use the clues to fill in the words.

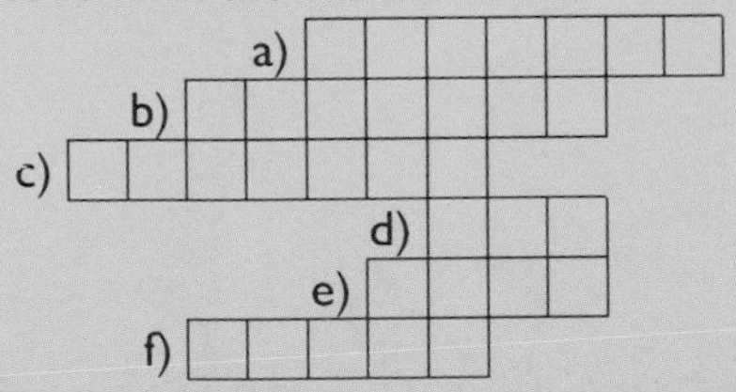
a)
b)
c)
d)
e)
f)

a) Most towns had one.
b) Very popular reading.
c) Cross this river for college.
d) After going round the shops.
e) You don't need to bring this nowadays.
f) A language learned at the grammar school.

Now find a word reading downwards and write a sentence about it.

2 Read source C.

a) Do you think James Murray is worried about his daughter's education? Explain your answer.

b) If he complained to the headmistress, what reasons might she give for her ways of educating the girls?

3 A pupil from one of Boston's colonial grammar schools has somehow turned up at your school for a day.

a) Make a list of the things about your school which might surprise or puzzle this boy.

b) How would you explain to him about the things on the list?

c) Make a list of things which happen in your school which he may understand, because they also happen in his own school.

5 RELIGION IN THE THIRTEEN COLONIES

The 16th century was a very troubled time for the Church in Europe. In England, Henry VIII separated the English Church from the Roman Catholic Church. Later, his daughter Mary brought England back into the Catholic Church. Later still, under his second daughter, Elizabeth, the English Church became separate again. In Germany, Martin Luther, followed by others, broke away from the Roman Catholic Church.

The religious changes caused wars. Most rulers suspected that people who did not worship in the same ways as themselves might be traitors. They would not allow other religious views, particularly if they were very unusual.

People did not want to change their ways of worshipping every time they had a new king or queen. Some felt so strongly that they sailed to America to gain their religious freedom.

The Puritans arrived first in 1620, on board the *Mayflower*. They settled in Plymouth, just south of modern Boston. More followed and they founded Massachusetts Bay. They liked a very simple sort of church service.

In their new life the church was the most important thing. When one clergyman, Roger Williams, suggested that they should let people worship in other ways, the Massachusetts Puritans were very angry and forced him to leave. However, as the years passed, they became less strict.

A The Shakers were an unusual religious group who went to America. They worshipped God in a strange shaking dance, and they did not believe in marriage.

It was different in the Middle Colonies. Swedes, Dutch, Germans and British all settled there. There were so many religions there that they all had to put up with each other.

B Around 1770 De Crèvecoeur, a French traveller, wrote this about settlers in the Middle Colonies:

In the house to the right, lives a Catholic, who prays to God as he has been taught . . . he works hard, raises wheat, he has a large family of children. His prayers offend nobody.

About one mile further along the same road, his next neighbour may be a good honest plodding German Lutheran.

How does it concern the . . . country . . . what [a] man's religious [feelings] are? He is a good farmer, he is a peaceable citizen.

C William Penn, the Quaker founder of Pennsylvania, making a treaty with Indians in 1763. He promised to let them keep their land. The painting is by Benjamin West.

D John Woolman, a Quaker, wrote of how, aged 23, in 1743, he realised slavery was wrong:

My employer, having a negro woman, sold her, and desired me to write a bill of sale. I said before my master . . . that I believed slavekeeping . . . [did not go with] the Christian religion.

(Woolman later took the lead in a campaign which freed slaves held by Quakers.)

Further south the first settlers belonged to the Church of England. Then they were joined by Scotch-Irish Presbyterians. The first Governor of Georgia invited the Methodist, John Wesley, to go out to preach. Many Georgians became Methodists. Slaves often found Methodism a great comfort, especially the hymn singing.

RELIGIONS IN EIGHTEENTH-CENTURY AMERICA
PURITANS liked a simple service.
LUTHERANS followed a German monk called Martin Luther who broke away from the Church of Rome.
QUAKERS were peaceful people. They had a meeting house instead of a church and they did not have priests.
The METHODIST church was started by John Wesley. Methodists enjoyed singing in their services.
ROMAN CATHOLICS looked to the Pope as their leader.
All those in favour?
CONGREGATIONALISTS let the people of the church make the decisions.
ANGLICANS are members of the Church of England started by Henry VIII in 1534 after his argument with the Pope.
BAPTISTS think people should not be baptised as babies, but should wait until they are old enough to make up their own minds.

E Religions in 18th-century America.

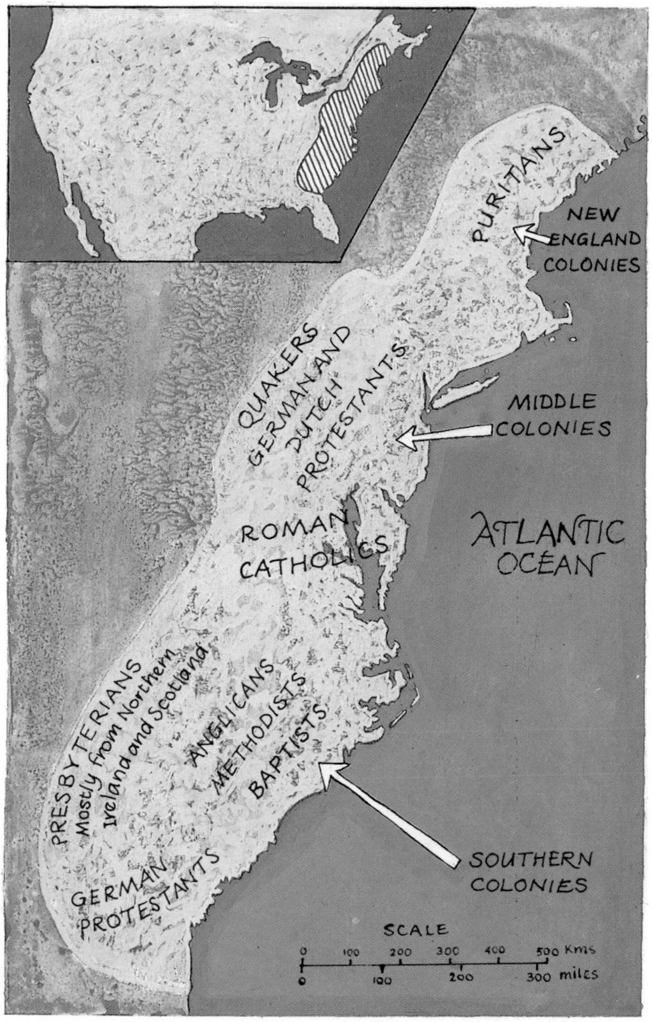
PURITANS
NEW ENGLAND COLONIES
QUAKERS GERMAN AND DUTCH PROTESTANTS
MIDDLE COLONIES
ROMAN CATHOLICS
ATLANTIC OCEAN
PRESBYTERIANS Mostly from Northern Ireland and Scotland
ANGLICANS
METHODISTS
BAPTISTS
SOUTHERN COLONIES
GERMAN PROTESTANTS
SCALE
0 100 200 300 400 500 Kms
0 100 200 300 miles

F Where the religions had most members.

1 a) Why do you think the Puritans were so angry with Roger Williams?
b) Were they right? Give your reasons.
c) Suppose you were starting up a new colony. How much freedom would you give to people? Discuss your ideas with other members of the class.

2 a) Look at source A. Give two reasons why some people might find the Shakers strange.
b) Look at sources C and D. Give two reasons why some Quakers might annoy other colonists.

3 a) Read source B. Does De Crèvecoeur think that settlers in the Middle Colonies mind about each other's religion or not?
b) What does he think is more important than a settler's religion?

4 a) Look at source E. Which of these religions shown have churches near you?
b) Use the religions named in sources E and F to make your own crossword or wordsearch puzzle. Then get your neighbour to solve it, and to write a sentence about each religion you name in the puzzle.

6 TOWNS AND HOUSES

A Philadelphia in the mid-18th century.

There were four main towns in the colonies – Boston, New York, Philadelphia and Charleston. Their buildings were as good as those in most British cities of the time. By 1758 the people of Philadelphia even had paved streets, thanks to a lottery which raised £2,250. Most towns had street lighting. If you were caught vandalising the New York lights you got 20 lashes or a £2.50 fine.

B In 1756, a British naval officer wrote home about New York:

I had no idea of finding a place in America consisting of near 2,000 houses elegantly built of brick, and the streets paved and spacious.

C Peter Kalm, a Swedish visitor to Philadelphia in 1748, wrote:

The streets are pretty and broad. [Philadelphia is as good as] the most ancient towns in Europe.

These towns had been built by craftsmen whose families had come from Europe. They had continued to use the best building ideas from their homelands, just changing them where necessary to suit America.

A visitor from England would have felt at home in Massachusetts and other parts of New England. Most houses there were wooden. A covering of small stones or wooden boarding called clapboarding gave protection. There were many similar houses in England, although the English sometimes used plaster or tiles for extra protection.

Some colonists, particularly in the south, had made fortunes as merchants, or as planters of indigo or tobacco. Their houses were much grander. They usually sent to London for books written by British architects.

One book, written by James Gibbs in 1728, was especially popular. It was meant to be used as a pattern book for country people to choose new houses.

D Monticello, a house in Virginia, built in the late 18th century. It was designed by the owner, Thomas Jefferson. He had travelled in Italy and admired the old buildings there. He designed his house in the same style.

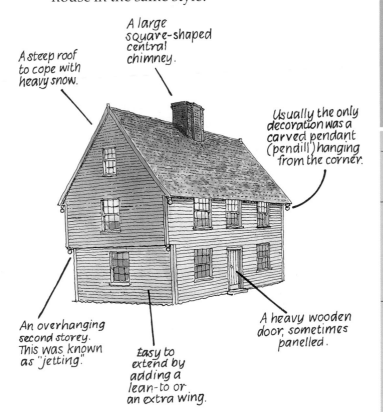

A large square-shaped central chimney.
A steep roof to cope with heavy snow.
Usually the only decoration was a carved pendant (pendill) hanging from the corner.
An overhanging second storey. This was known as "jetting."
Easy to extend by adding a lean-to or an extra wing.
A heavy wooden door, sometimes panelled.

E A typical New England 18th-century house.

Peter Kalm and the British officer were surprised to find New York and Philadelphia as good as the best towns in Europe. Historians would not be so surprised. Although they expect to find changes in the things they study, they also expect to find that many things stay the same.

1 Look at source A. What things in the picture may have helped Peter Kalm form his good impression of Philadelphia?

2 Work in pairs. Look at source E.
a) List ways in which your own homes are similar to this house.
b) Now list ways in which they are different.
c) Think of possible reasons for the similarities and differences.

3 Look at source D.
a) Why would it be difficult to build a house like this in the 18th century?
b) Whom do you suppose did most of the hard work?
c) There were more of these very big houses in the southern colonies than in the north. Write down as many reasons as you can why this might be so.

7 MUSIC AND ART

The colonists liked music. Older New Englanders often met in each other's houses in the evenings to sing religious songs. Young people preferred ballads . One of these was called 'The Two Faithful Lovers'. Harvard College students used to carry the words of it inside the covers of their notebooks.

On page 11 there is a picture of slaves making music after their work in the fields was done. They sang during their work as well. It was a way of making it a little easier.

Although most colonists didn't take black music seriously, it was going to have a big influence on later types of American music, such as jazz, blues, and rock 'n' roll.

The white colonists sang many tunes that were popular in Britain, although they often gave these tunes different words. One of these, 'Yankee Doodle', became a national song.

A *A Boy with a Squirrel* by J.S. Copley.

Of course, Americans were composing songs of their own as well as singing songs from Britain. They were painting good pictures as well. In 1766 the great British painter, Sir Joshua Reynolds, got quite a surprise when he saw source A, painted by a young Boston man.

B Sir Joshua said about the picture:
It is a WONDERFUL picture to be sent by a young man who was never out of New England and had only some bad copies to study.

Sir Joshua had been shown the picture by an American painter called Benjamin West. (You saw one of his paintings on page 14.) West had started to paint when he was very young. He made his first brushes from the moulting fur of the family cats!

He went to paint in London, and worked for the king at Windsor Castle. He helped lots of young American painters, letting them stay at his house.

Patience Lovell Wright was one of the most adventurous American artists. Her husband died in 1769 and she had to earn money to keep her family. She decided she might make more money from waxwork modelling than from painting. Abigail Adams visited her exhibition in London in the 1780s.

C Abigail Adams wrote in a letter:
I went to see the celebrated Mrs Wright. There was an old clergyman sitting reading a paper in the middle of the room. I was [taken in] by this figure for ten minutes, and was finally told that it was only wax.

Mrs Wright actually earned her living as an artist, but most American housewives were also very artistic. They made marvellous patchwork quilts. Even the poorest families had at least one, which was handed down as an heirloom . This wasn't something new in America. Indian women had been making beautifully patterned cloth and pottery for hundreds of years.

D A colonial quilt.

E An Indian woman demonstrating traditional basketry work.

1 a) Do you think the older New Englanders would approve of what the Harvard students scribbled in their exercise books? Give reasons.
b) How many members of your class have words of songs hidden anywhere in their notebooks?
c) Do teachers usually approve of this habit? Give reasons.
d) What does this tell you about how things change or stay the same?

2 a) Study source B. Did Sir Joshua Reynolds think that America was an exciting place for a painter? How do you know?
b) Look at source A. Make a list of reasons why Sir Joshua may have thought it was a good picture.

3 a) Look at source D. Write down two possible reasons why American women made quilts like this.
b) Design either your own pattern for a quilt, or an Indian style pattern.

8 SONS OF LIBERTY

1495 1550 1600 1650 1700 1750 1800

In 1763 the long wars against the French in North America came to an end. Britain gained much new land. This now needed organising. It also needed defending, because there was always the chance that the French would try to take their revenge.

Taxes in Britain were already high. So the Government decided that the colonists should pay something towards their own defence. Over the next few years, Britain tried several times to get them to do this.

In 1765, for example, a Stamp Act was passed by the British Parliament. All colonial legal documents and newspapers were to carry a special stamp tax. This tax was to be used to pay an army to defend the colonies against either the Indians or the French.

The colonists flatly refused to use the stamps. They did not see why people in London should decide what taxes they had to pay. Anyway, now the war was over, work was difficult to find and many colonists were very hard up.

Secret groups, called the Sons of Liberty, sprang up to lead the protests. They worked out ways of persuading those men who had applied to be Stamp Agents to change their minds. The Daughters of Liberty formed groups as well. They were determined not to buy British goods, and worked hard producing homespun cloth.

Most newspaper owners were Daughters or Sons of Liberty. They made sure that everyone knew what was happening.

The Protests led to a Stamp Act Congress, which met in New York with representatives from eight colonies. The Congress decided that they, too, would stop buying British goods.

It was a good move. By June 1766 worried London merchants had persuaded the Government to repeal the Stamp Act. The colonists were delighted.

A The Stamp Act is 'buried'. An English cartoon in 1766. On the coffin it says, 'Born in 1765. Died in 1766.'

1715
1745
CONWAY
ROCKINGHAM
GRAFTON
Manchester
Halifax
Leeds
Liverpool
Sheffield and Birm
Goods now Shipd

This has to be glued here!!

The TIMES are Dreadful, Diſmal Doleful Dolorous, and DOLLAR-LESS.
An Emblem of the Effects of the STAMP
O! the fatal Stamp
Thurſday, October 31, 1765.
THE
NUMB. 1195.
PENNSYLVANIA JOURNAL;
AND
WEEKLY ADVERTISER.
EXPIRING: In Hopes of a Reſurrection to LIFE again.

B The skull and crossbones (top right) appeared in this newspaper in 1765 as a warning not to use the stamps.

C John Rowe, a Boston merchant, described in his diary for 1765 how a warning was given to Andrew Oliver, the Boston Stamp Officer.

Aug. 14. A Great Number of People assembled this morning to see [a model of] the Stamp Officer hung on Deacon Elliot's tree. This stamp officer hung up all Day – at night they cut him down and carried in Triumph amidst the [cheers] of many thousands who were gathered together on that occasion.

They pulled down a New Building which some people thought was [to be] for a Stamp Office and did some mischief to Mr Andrew Oliver's house.

Aug. 16. Heard that Mr Andrew Oliver had resigned his [post]. There was great Rejoicing last evening in Boston.

D Peter Oliver, a Massachusetts judge, and Andrew's brother, gave his version of what happened. He wrote this in London in 1781.

[Andrew Oliver] who was appointed a Stamp Master, was attacked, and his House much damaged. He was carried to the Tree of Liberty by the Mob & there he was obliged, on Pain of Death, to [promise] to resign his Office.

E A poster, probably published by Editor Holt of the *New York Postboy*, which appeared around New York on the night of 21 October 1765:

The first man that either distributes or makes use of the stamp paper, let him take care of his House, Person & Effects. The voice of the people. We dare.

F John Holt, printer of the *New York Gazette* and the *Postboy*, wrote in 1765 to tell Mrs Benjamin Franklin in Philadelphia about protests in New York when two merchants decided to use the stamps.

By ten o'clock I suppose 2,000 people attended at the Coffee House, among them most of the principal men in Town – The Culprits' apologies did not satisfy the people . . . and the Sons of Liberty found it necessary to use their influence. One or two men, attended by about a thousand others, were then sent for the stamps, which were brought to the Coffee House, and the merchant who had used them was ordered himself to kindle the fire and [burn] them.

A historian is not often lucky enough to be able to find the whole truth about an event written down by one person. Usually she or he will have to read more than one account, and then piece together what really happened.

1. Read sources C and D.
   a) What does John Rowe say happened to Andrew Oliver?
   b) What does Peter Oliver say happened?
   c) Decide what probably really happened. Give reasons for your view.
2. Design a poster for the Daughters or the Sons of Liberty, warning people against using the new stamps.
3. Read source F. Then look again at sources C, D and E. Make a list of ways in which the Sons of Liberty may have persuaded people not to use the stamps.
4. Look at source A. How can you tell that the artist is making fun of the Stamp Act?
5. How might each of the following people have felt about the Stamp Act? Give your reasons.
   a) A family living on the edge of Indian territory;
   b) A London merchant;
   c) A colonial newspaper editor;
   d) An out-of-work colonist;
   e) A British taxpayer.

9 DAUGHTERS OF LIBERTY

In the 18th century, American women lived in a man's world. A single woman was under her father's control. A married woman and her property were under her husband's control.

Husbands believed that their wives' place was at home, raising children and looking after them. There was certainly plenty to keep women busy at home, particularly if they couldn't afford help.

A An 18th-century American family – quite a small one by the standards of the time.

B Mrs Mary Gibson Tilghmann, aged 24, with her sons, painted by Charles Willson Peake (1789). She died a year later.

Having children was a risky business. Although the midwives were skilled, out of every 30 births at least one mother died. It was quite common for a man to have buried four wives before the fifth buried him.

In the 17th century, strong-minded New England women had often been accused of being witches. Those times were past, but having strong opinions on religion or politics was still not liked. The Daughters of Liberty organisations must have been quite a breakthrough.

Black American women were in an even worse situation. Most of them lived on plantations in the south as slaves. Slave owners liked them to have lots of children because that meant more workers for them. There was always the chance that the children, particularly teenagers, could be sold to another owner, and the family broken up.

Most white American men had a low opinion of Indian women. Yet they were often freer than the white men's own wives. Although they worked hard, they shared the work with their husbands and they could become leaders of the tribe. However, the Indian women's rights to be leaders began to die because white men refused to parley with them.

In spite of these drawbacks women progressed. In the countryside they worked hard alongside their menfolk. In the towns some women ran important businesses. They were merchants; they owned newspapers and shops; they ran post offices and inns. During the Revolution they would seize the opportunity to do even more.

C The Reverend Benjamin Colman in a sermon in Boston (1715):

A mother with a train of children after her is one of the most admirable and lovely sights in the visible Creation of God.

D Thomas Clap, President of Yale College, at his wife's funeral in 1736:

She would sometimes say to me that Bearing, tending and Burying Children was Hard work, and that She Had Done a great Deal of it for one of Her Age. (She Had 6 children whereof she buried 4 and Dyed in ye 24 year of Her Age.) Yet she would Say it was the work She was made for, and what God had Called Her to.

E Part of a day in the life of Abigail Foote in 1695:

Fix'd gown for Prude. Mend Mother's Riding-hood – spun short thread – Fix'd two gowns for Welsh's girls – spun linen – worked on cheese basket – pleated and ironed – Read a sermon of Doddridge's – milked the cows – spun linen – Set a red dye – Had two scholars from Mrs Taylor's – [prepared] two Pounds of whole wool – spun harness twine – cleaned the pewter.

G Eliza Wilkinson wrote to a friend in 1782:

The men say we have no business with [politics]. I won't have it thought that we are capable of nothing more than minding the dairy, visiting the poultry-house and all such domestic concerns. Surely we have sense enough to give our opinions . . . without being reminded of our spinning and household affairs as the only matters we are capable of thinking or speaking of.

You probably agree that things have changed for women since the 18th century. A historian wants to know how things have changed, and how much they have changed.

F Harvard College, embroidered by a woman in about 1765. It was the nearest she would get to a college education.

1 Read source C. Look at sources A and B. Do you agree with the Reverend Colman? Give reasons.

2 Read source D. Do you think that Thomas Clap loved his wife? How did you decide?

3 Read sources E and G.
a) Was Abigail an educated girl? Give your reasons.
b) What is Eliza really complaining about?
c) Did things seem to have changed much for women between 1695 and 1782? Explain how you decided.

4 a) Prepare a list of questions to ask your parents, teachers and friends so that you can find out their ideas about the rights of women today.
b) In a group compare the answers you receive and try to work out the reasons for any differences.
c) In what ways have women made progress since the days of the Daughters of Liberty?
d)Are any of the problems faced by modern women the same as those faced by the colonial women? Explain your answer.

WHO WAS TO BLAME?

A Hiller B. Zobel, a modern historian who probably read most sources about the event, wrote in 1970:

Richard Hirons, the doctor, lived on the east side of Brattle Street. Shortly after 8pm Dr Hirons noticed considerable activity in Brattle Street: soldiers variously armed with bayonets, clubs and 'one thing and another' were passing back and forth. After ten minutes of this, a man rushed . . . toward Brattle Street, shouting loudly, 'Town born, turn out! Town born, turn out!' . . .

Through narrow Draper's Passage now poured a crowd, whether civilian or military, Hirons could not tell. Armed with clubs and sticks, they thumped the sides of the passage so [hard] that Hirons locked his door, [put out] his front lights, and went upstairs to watch . . .

Boston had no fire [brigade]. In the event of fire the largely wooden-built town depended on volunteers. When a church bell rang the alarm Bostonians hurried to the site. Some manned the wheeled pumps which were housed in convenient central [places] around the town. Others brought bags to help the families save their belongings and leather buckets to help carry water.

Bells might ring in the daytime for joy or mourning. But in the night, an off hour church bell meant only one thing. [So] when sometime after 9pm, first the Brattle Street Church bells, then those of the Old Brick [Church] began to peal, [the townspeople knew what to do]. Fire, fire, fire, they shouted.

B Boston in 1770.

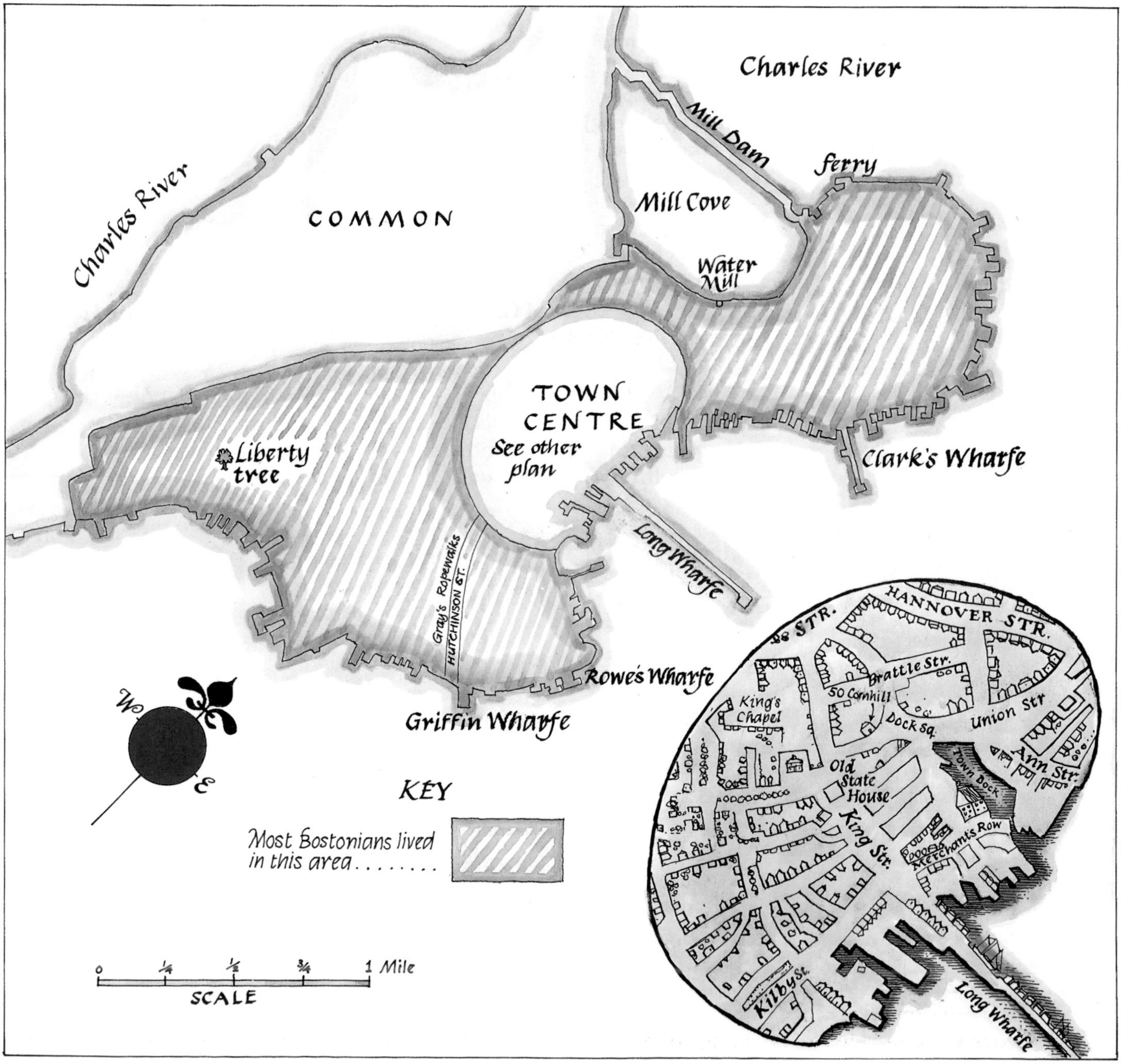

Charles River
Mill Dam
Ferry
Mill Cove
Charles River
COMMON
Water Mill
TOWN CENTRE
See other plan
Liberty tree
Clark's Wharfe
Long Wharfe
Gray's Ropewalks
HUTCHINSON ST.
Rowe's Wharfe
Griffin Wharfe
KEY
Most Bostonians lived in this area . . . .
0 ¼ ½ ¾ 1 Mile
SCALE
HANNOVER STR.
STR.
Brattle Str.
King's Chapel
50 Cornhill
Dock Sq.
Union Str
Town Dock
Ann Str.
Old State House
King Str.
Merchants Row
Kilby St.
Long Wharfe

C Evidence given at Preston's trial by Andrew, a black slave.

Andrew told the court how the barber's boy taunted a soldier called Montgomery shouting 'Damn you bloody back lobster! Are you going to stab me?'

A crowd came down King Street led by a very tall black man with a stick. This must have been Crispus Attucks.

This man swung the stick first at Preston, then at Montgomery. The crowd shouted, 'Kill him! Knock him over!'

Preston was standing out in front of his men, looking at the crowd, with his back to Andrew. A voice different from the rest cried, 'Fire!' and the first gun went off. Although Andrew could not see Preston's face, he was 'certain the voice came from beyond him.'

D The Old State House in King Street as it is today. (Now State Street.) You can see it in Paul Revere's engraving on page 25. The picture of George Hewes now hangs here.

E Statement given to the court by Oliver Wendell, Andrew's master.

Andrew has lived with me ten years. His character for truth . . . and understanding is good. He can read and write.

F Dr John Jeffries told of his conversation with Patrick Carr just before his death.

I asked him whether he thought the soldiers would have been hurt, if they had not fired. He said he really thought they would, for he heard many voices cry out, kill them. I asked him whether he thought they fired in self-defence, or on purpose to destroy the people. He said he really thought they did fire to defend themselves, that he did not blame the man whoever he was, that shot him.

A Corporal with his Brown Bess flintlock musket.

1 Read source A.
a) Does what Dr Hirons saw and heard make you think that the townspeople or the soldiers started the fight? Explain how you decided.
b) Was Dr Hirons frightened? Give a reason for your answer.
c) Why do you think Hiller Zobel explained about the Boston fire alarm system?
d) Does any other source indicate that some townspeople might think there was a fire? Explain your answer.

2 Read sources C and E.
a) Why do you think Andrew had no surname?
b) Why do you think his master was called to give evidence about him?

3 In groups, look at all the sources and use them to puzzle out what may have happened. Try to decide about things like this:
a) Was the fight caused by youths, or was there more to it?
b) Did the townspeople decide to get the soldiers or was it the other way round?
c) Do you think the Captain gave an order to fire? If not, then what do you think happened?
d) When you have decided, explain your ideas to the rest of the class.

11 THE BOSTON TEA PARTY

1495 1550 1600 1650 1700 1750 1800

Captain Preston was tried for murder and found not guilty – but many Bostonians still thought it had been a massacre. Every 5 March they held ceremonies to keep the bitter memories alive.

Many people went on refusing to buy British goods, particularly tea. This meant that the East India Company, which shipped the tea from India, was losing a lot of money. The British Prime Minister, Lord North, hit on an idea to help the company.

In 1773 his Tea Act became law. The East India Company was to be allowed to ship its tea direct to America. Tea would be so cheap that smuggling would not be worthwhile. Boston people were furious. They felt the Government was trying to get round their tea ban.

On Sunday, 28 November 1773 the ship *Dartmouth* arrived, carrying 114 chests of tea. The Boston Sons of Liberty, led by Sam Adams, put up notices on every street corner.

A The Green Dragon Tavern in Union Street, where the Boston Sons of Liberty used to make their plans.

B From John Rowe's diary.
Nov. 29 This morning there were papers stuck up [saying] 'Friends, [Brothers], Countrymen! The hated Tea, ship'd for this Port by the East India Company is now arriv'd. Every Friend to his Country is now called upon to meet at Faneuil Hall at nine of Clock this Day'.

So many turned up that the meeting had to be moved to the Old South Meeting House. They voted that Mr Rotch, the owner's agent, must take the tea straight back to England. A guard was put on the *Dartmouth* and two other tea ships at Griffin's Wharf.

C Edward G. Porter, a Boston historian writing in 1882, continued the story:
On the eleventh of December [Mr Rotch] was asked why he had not kept his agreement to send the tea back. He replied that it was out of his power to do so. No vessel was allowed to put to sea without [Governor Hutchinson's permission]. The Guns at the castle were loaded, and Admiral Montagu had sent two warships to guard the passages out of the harbour.

The writer in source C was not alive at the time of the Boston Tea Party, so his account is a secondary, not a primary source. It can still be very useful when we are studying the Boston Tea Party, if the writer has based the account on primary sources.

1 Read source C.
a) Make a list of ways in which Edward Porter may have got information about what happened.
b) Why might he have found it easier than a modern historian to find out about the tea party? Explain your answer.

On 16 December another meeting was called. About 7,000 people turned up. Mr Rotch rode out to the Governor's country home in a last attempt to get permission to sail. At 5:45pm he returned with the news that the Governor still refused.

This is what George Hewes remembered happening next: Sam Adams said, 'This meeting can do nothing more to save the country.'

These words must have been a signal. People in the gallery started to shout, 'To Griffin's Wharf! Boston Harbour a teapot tonight!' Everyone rushed out of the Meeting House hooting, and making Indian noises. 'The Mohawks are coming!' some of them shouted.

John Andrews, a merchant, was at his house three blocks away. He rushed to the Old South Meeting House when he heard the noise and was nearly knocked over as the crowds poured out.

E The Boston Tea Party.

D George Hewes continues the story. (Talking to Thatcher, the journalist, in 1835.)

I covered my face and hands with coaldust in the shop of a blacksmith. I fell in with men who were dressed, equipped and painted as I was and marched to [Griffin's Wharf]. When we arrived the commander of [my] division [put me in charge], and ordered me to go to the captain and demand the keys to the hatches, take out the chests of tea, and throw them overboard, first cutting and splitting the chests with our tomahawks.

Who actually destroyed the tea was kept a secret. Benjamin Edes, the printer, had a list which he kept locked in his desk. When he died, another Son of Liberty came and took it away. It hasn't been seen since. But we know Thomas Melvill was there. His family still have the tea which was found in his boots next morning!

2

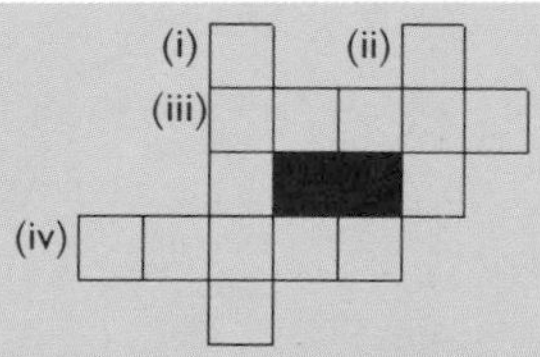

(i)
(ii)
(iii)
(iv)

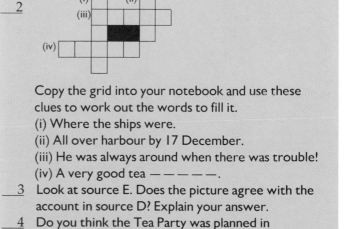

Copy the grid into your notebook and use these clues to work out the words to fill it.

(i) Where the ships were.

(ii) All over harbour by 17 December.

(iii) He was always around when there was trouble!

(iv) A very good tea — — — — —.

3 Look at source E. Does the picture agree with the account in source D? Explain your answer.

4 Do you think the Tea Party was planned in advance? Make a list of reasons for your answer.

12 BOSTON PAYS FOR THE PARTY

1495 1550 1600 1650 1700 1750 1800

Early next day Paul Revere rode off on an 11-day trip to New York and Philadelphia, with letters about Boston's Tea Party. This trip was the first of many. People in different colonies were forming letter-writing clubs to keep in touch.

He brought back news that the Sons of Liberty in both places supported what Boston had done. They had also started to plan action against tea ships expected any day in their own ports.

A In October 1773 the Philadelphia Committee for Tarring and Feathering issued this warning to the captain of an expected ship:

What think you, Captain, of a [rope] round your neck, ten gallons of Liquid Tar on your [head], with the feathers of a dozen wild Geese [put] over that, to [improve] your appearance?

B Peter Oliver described tarring and feathering in 1781:

First, strip a person naked, then heat the tar until it is thin, pour it upon the naked Flesh. Sprinkle upon the Tar, while it is yet warm, as many Feathers as will stick to it. Then hold a lighted candle to the Feathers, & try to set it all on fire. Take also a [rope] and put it round the person's neck.

45
45

C A victim of tarring and feathering in 1774.

Tarring and feathering had been a punishment in England since the 12th century. Americans first used it as fancy dress on 5 November. Then it became a punishment, but it was more likely to be threatened than carried out.

Source C shows Johnny Malcolm, a Boston customs informer. On a freezing January night he was carted around for four hours, whipped, and forced to drink the king's health in gallons of tea until he almost burst.

The crowd pretended to cut off his ears and to hang him. At last, half-frozen, he was rolled out of the cart like a log. His flesh was peeling off his back like pieces of wood.

Captain Ayres, on board the *Polly*, arrived in Philadelphia on Christmas Day 1774 carrying tea. He set sail back to England very quickly without unloading.

1 Study sources A, B and C.
a) Why do you think the captain of the teaship did not unload the tea?
b) Do you think tarring and feathering was a good punishment? Give your reasons.
c) It was not used often. Why do you think this was?

New York also took action against its teaships. King George III and Lord North were angry. They thought that Boston had gone too far. They ordered Governor Hutchinson back to London to tell them about the situation. The British Parliament passed an Act closing the port of Boston until the tea was paid for. General Gage took over as Governor.

Moderate Americans at first agreed with the king. However, after the harbour was closed, they began to have second thoughts. They realised that what happened to Boston one day might happen to them the next.

When Americans heard about the Quebec Act which the British Parliament passed in 1774, they worried even more. Before 1763 the French and the British had fought each other in North America for many years. The British had defeated the French, but there were still many French settlers in Canada.

The Quebec Act said that these French settlers were to have their French laws, their language and their Roman Catholic religion officially accepted.

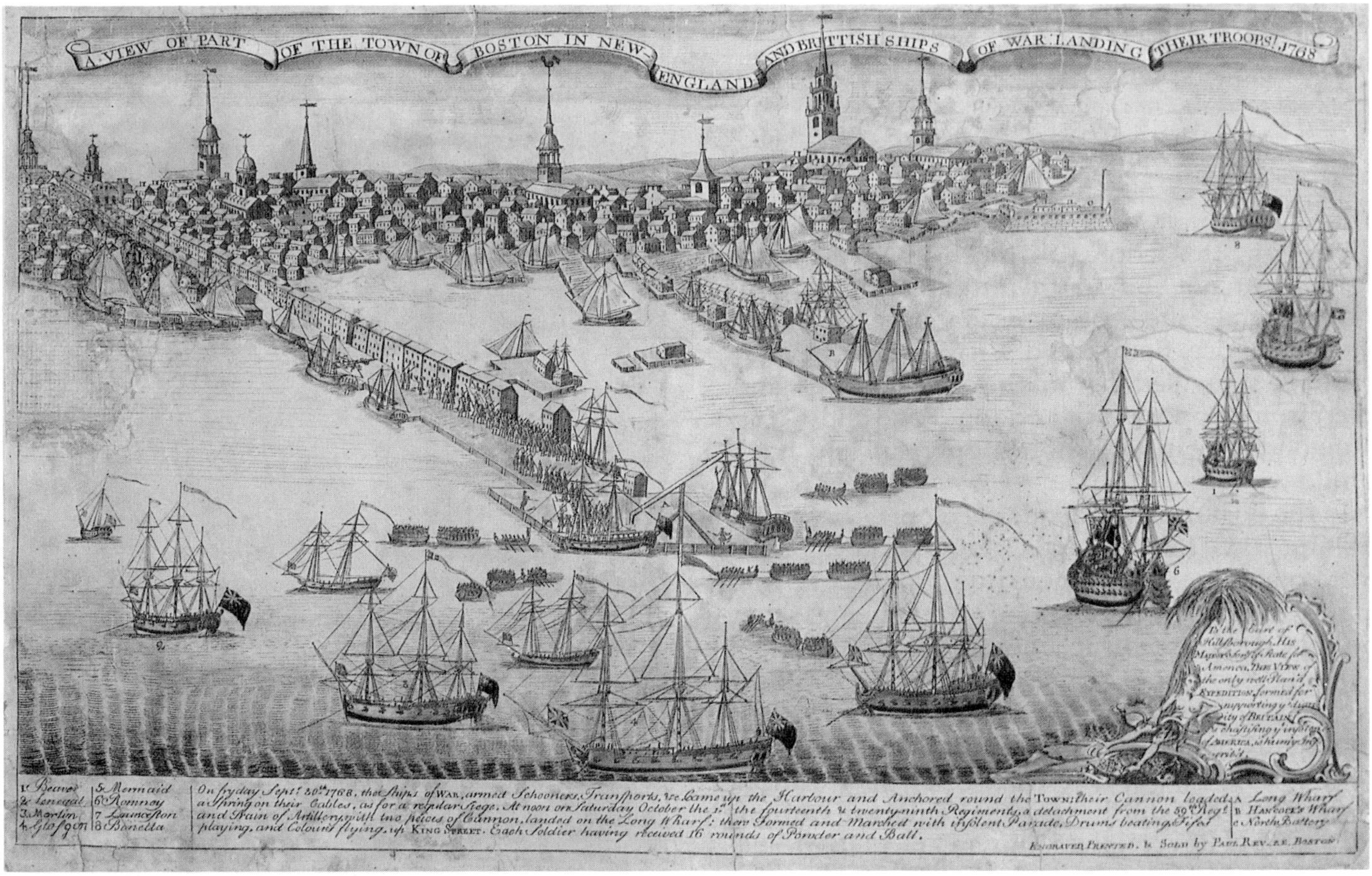
A VIEW OF PART OF THE TOWN OF BOSTON IN NEW-ENGLAND AND BRITTISH SHIPS OF WAR: LANDING THEIR TROOPS! 1768
1 Beaver 2 Senegal 3 Martin 4 Glasgow
5 Mermaid 6 Romney 7 Launceston 8 Bonetta
On fryday Sept. 30th 1768, the Ships of WAR, armed Schooners, Transports, &c. Came up the Harbour and Anchored round the TOWN; their Cannon loaded, a Spring on their Cables, as for a regular Siege. At noon on Saturday October the 1st the fourteenth & twenty-ninth Regiments, a detachment from the 59th Regt. and Train of Artillery, with two pieces of Cannon, landed on the Long Wharf; there Formed and Marched with insolent Parade, Drums beating, Fifes playing, and Colours flying, up KING STREET. Each Soldier having received 16 rounds of Powder and Ball.
A Long Wharf
B Hancock's Wharf
C North Battery
Engraved, Printed, & Sold by PAUL REVERE, BOSTON

D British troops coming ashore in Boston in 1768 to protect the customs commissioners.

Many colonists remembered that their grandparents had left Europe to escape from that same Catholic religion.

The Quebec Act also moved the Canadian border right down to the Ohio River. Some colonists had hoped to make money selling land around the Ohio River. The new Act made this impossible.

The letter-writing clubs organised a conference in Philadelphia – a Continental Congress. All the colonies except Georgia sent representatives to discuss the problems. John Adams and his cousin Sam went for Massachusetts. Virginia sent Thomas Jefferson and George Washington.

__2__ You are an American. Up till now you have agreed with Lord North that tipping tea overboard should be punished. Make a list of reasons why you might change your mind after hearing about the closing of Boston Harbour and the Quebec Act.

__3__

S	H	I	P	A	Q
A		O	N	S	U
E	R	G	M	A	E
T	R	A		M	B
Y	D	R	A	T	E
A		T	C	A	C

Sam
Quebec Act
Teaship
Adams
Port
Tar

a) Copy the puzzle into your exercise book. Find the above words in the puzzle and ring them.
b) Write a sentence about each word.
c) The remaining letters spell how George III felt. Write the word down and explain why he felt that way.
d) Do you think he was right to feel that way? Explain your answer.

__4__ a) Look back at pages 8 and 9 to see how colonists in the north earned their livings.
b) Now look at source D. Do you think the port of Boston played a big part in the life of Boston people? Explain your answer.
c) Make a list of possible ways in which closing the port of Boston might affect the people.
d) You are a member of the Boston letter-writing club (the Committee of Correspondence). Write a letter to be taken to New York and Philadelphia by Paul Revere or another rider, explaining what has happened, how it is affecting Boston, and asking for help.

14 THE BATTLE OF LEXINGTON, 1775

1495 1550 1600 1650 1700 1750 1800

General Gage had been getting worried about the Minutemen. His spies told him that they were building up arms supplies at Concord. He planned a secret night expedition to seize them.

But it was hard to keep things secret in Boston. Paul Revere and his friends from the Green Dragon took turns to keep a careful watch.

A Much later, in 1798, Paul Revere wrote an account of what he did on the night of 18 April 1775.

I [had made an arrangement] with a Colonel Conant that if the British went out by water, we would show two lanterns in the North Church steeple; and if by land, one, as a signal. I called upon a friend, and [asked] him to [light the lanterns]. Two friends rowed me across Charles River.

Revere later told his children that he was so excited he forgot his spurs. He sent back his dog to get them from his wife, Rachel. It had a note pinned to its collar.

Colonel Conant had seen the lights and was waiting with a good horse. Off galloped Revere. At Medford he woke up the captain of the local Minutemen, and then he gave the alarm at every house on the road into Lexington.

There he warned Sam Adams and John Hancock. They were getting ready to leave for a congress in Philadelphia.

At Lexington he met up with Billy Dawes, who had come out by road across Boston Neck. They set off together for Concord, with a Dr Prescott. He was going home after visiting his Lexington girlfriend.

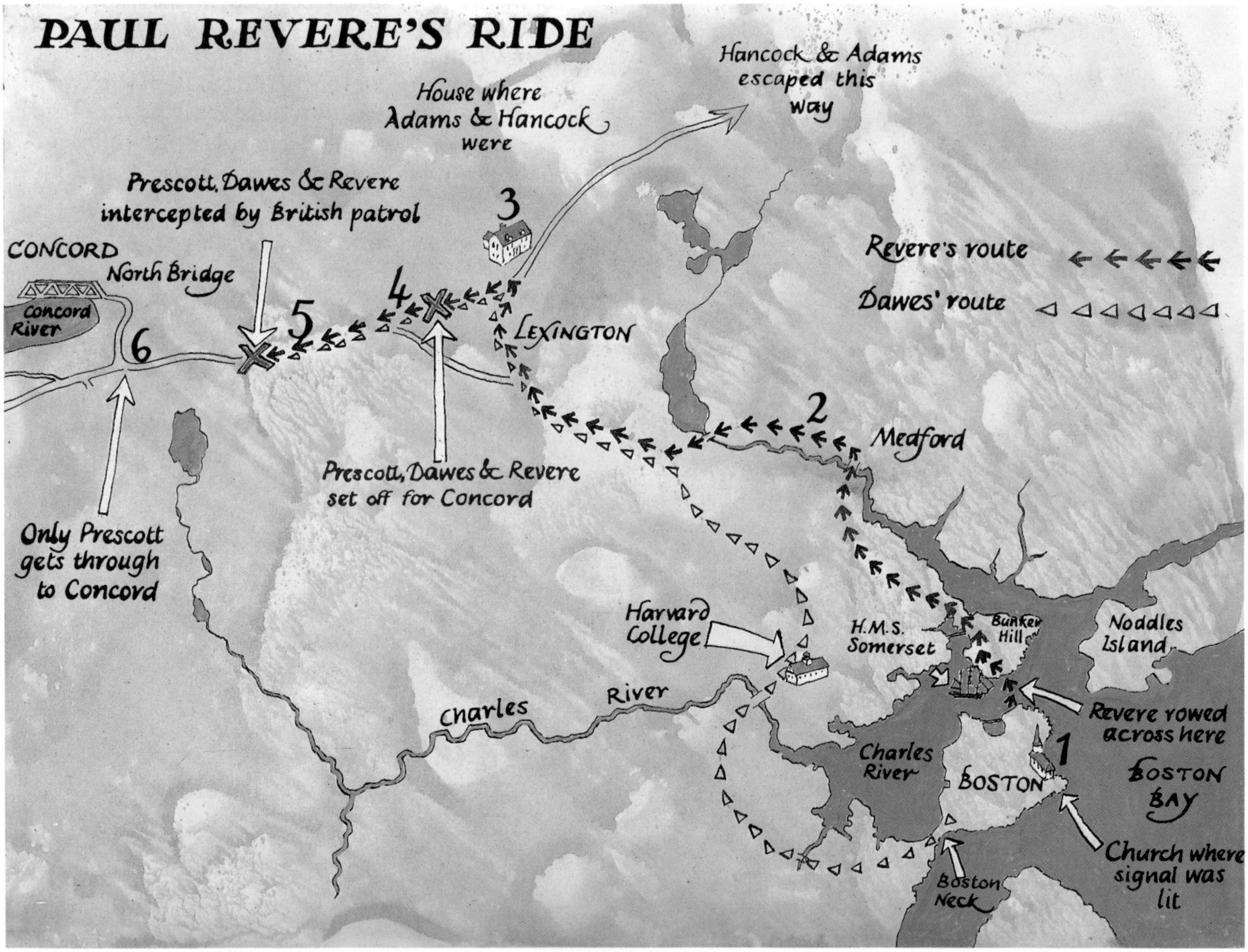

PAUL REVERE'S RIDE
Hancock & Adams escaped this way
House where Adams & Hancock were
Prescott, Dawes & Revere intercepted by British patrol
3
CONCORD
North Bridge
Concord River
6
5
4
LEXINGTON
Revere's route
Dawes' route
2
Medford
Prescott, Dawes & Revere set off for Concord
Only Prescott gets through to Concord
Harvard College
H.M.S. Somerset
Bunker Hill
Noddles Island
Charles
River
Reverе rowed across here
1
Charles River
BOSTON
BOSTON BAY
Church where signal was lit
Boston Neck

B Paul Revere's Ride.

C This picture by Amos Doolittle, drawn shortly afterwards, shows the scene described in source D.

Some Redcoats blocked their way, and only Dr Prescott managed to get through to warn his hometown.

By the time the Redcoats arrived in Lexington, about 60 Minutemen were ready on the green.

'Ye villains! Ye rebels! Lay down your arms!' thundered Major Pitcairn, the Redcoat leader.

No one was sure who fired first. But, when the shooting stopped, eight Americans lay dead. So began the war for American Independence.

The Redcoats carried on to Concord, but most of the ammunition had been hidden. They started back for Boston and the two sides met again at North Bridge. The Minutemen kept attacking, and it was a very tired British force that limped back to Boston.

D A British officer described the march back in his diary that night:

We were fired on from Houses and behind Trees. People hid themselves in Houses till we had passed, and then fired; the Country was full of Hills, Woods, stone Walls, &c, which the Rebels did not fail to take advantage of. In this way we marched between nine and ten miles, their numbers increasing while ours was reducing by deaths, wounds, and [tiredness].

E A historian called Donald Chidsey ended his work on the Battles of Lexington and Concord with these words:

The score: British 73 killed, 174 wounded; Americans 49 killed, 39 wounded. But there was a lot more to it than that.

If we have two sources about the same event we can compare them. If they seem reliable, we can use them together to find out what happened.

1 Study source B. There are six places numbered on the map. Write a sentence saying what happened at each place.

2 a) Why do you think no one wanted to admit that their side fired first at Lexington?
b) Read source E. What did Donald Chidsey mean?

3 a) Look at source C. Make a list of things the picture tells you about the British army's march back to Boston from Lexington.
b) Now read source D. Do the two sources agree? Give reasons for your answer.
c) Using both sources, write a paragraph describing the event.

16 THE BATTLE OF BUNKER HILL

1495 1550 1600 1650 1700 1750 1800

Times were hard in Boston after Lexington. American volunteers blockaded all land routes out of the town. The arrival by sea of British reinforcements led by Generals Howe, Clinton and Burgoyne must have been very welcome indeed.

All the troops in Boston were longing for action, but General Gage made no big plans. There were a few scraps on Noddles Island in the Bay, but nothing more. When the word got around that the British were going to break out and build forts on Bunker Hill and Dorchester Heights the Americans decided to get in first. Overnight they occupied Bunker Hill.

B John Barker, a British officer in Boston, wrote in his diary for 1775:

June 17th. At daybreak we were alarmed by the *Glasgow* (a British ship) firing. We found it was [firing] at the Rebels who were erecting a [fort] on the Heights of Charlestown. [A large company of soldiers] commanded by Majr. Genl. Howe set off about 1 o'clock and landed on the right of Charlestown.

Between 3 and 4 o'clock in the afternoon the whole marched to the attack [and made the Rebels] fly over the Neck which joins Charlestown to the Continent. Just about the beginning of the Attack the Town was set on fire and the whole burnt to Ashes.

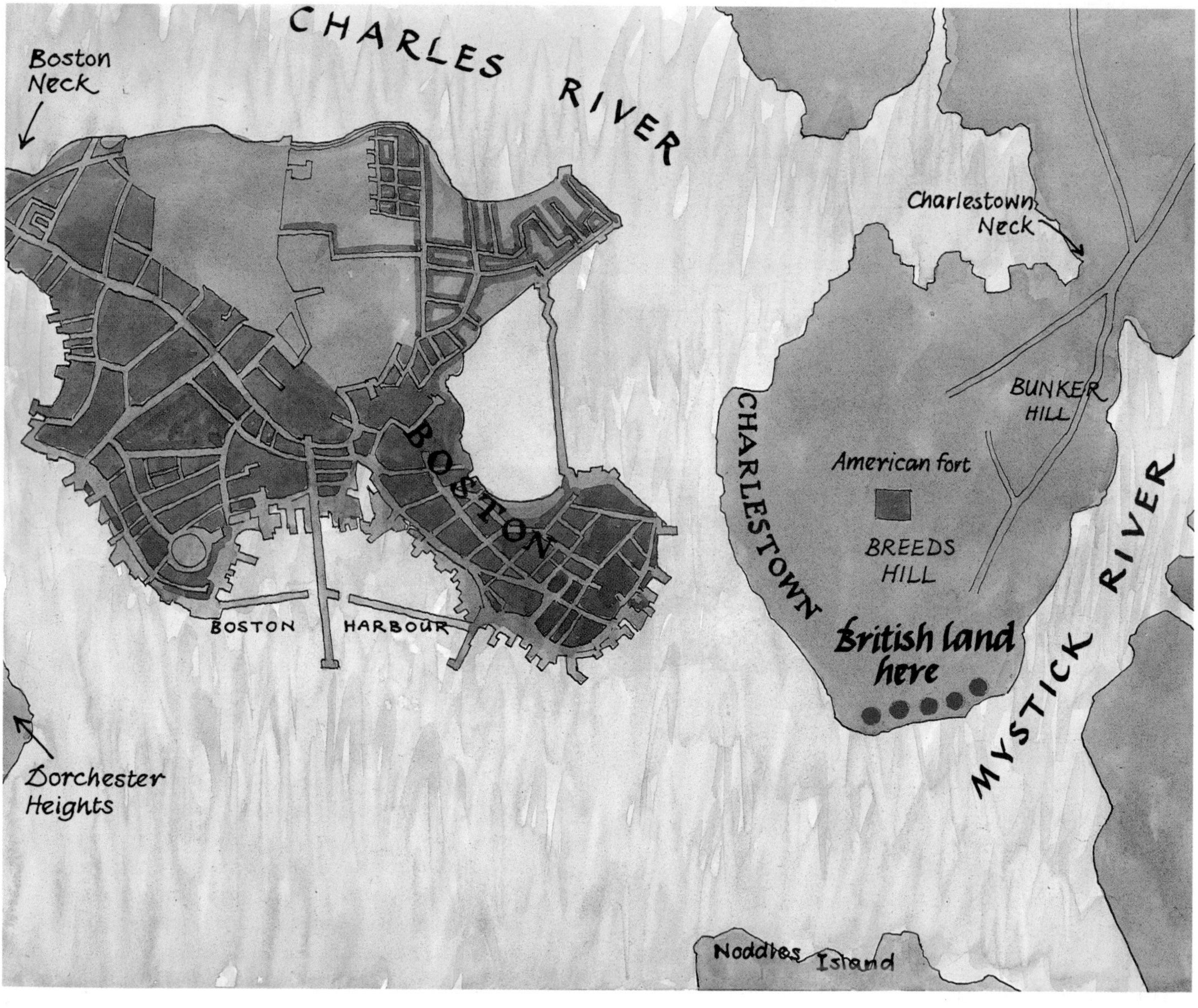

CHARLES RIVER
Boston Neck
Charlestown Neck
BUNKER HILL
CHARLESTOWN
BOSTON
American fort
BREEDS HILL
BOSTON HARBOUR
British land here
MYSTICK RIVER
Dorchester Heights
Noddles Island

A The area around Boston.

CHARLES TOWN
BOSTON

C Charlestown on fire during the Battle of Bunker Hill.

Lieutenant Barker made it all sound very matter-of-fact, but it was a very bloody battle. The British claimed victory because they drove the Americans off the hill. The Americans said they won because they killed or wounded so many British.

The Americans' estimated casualties were: 115 dead, 305 wounded and 30 missing. Amongst the dead was Dr Joseph Warren, Chairman of the Boston Committee of Safety. The British lost at least 226, with another 828 wounded.

D On Sunday, 18 June 1775, Abigail Adams wrote to her husband, John, from Weymouth just outside Boston. (He was at the Congress in Philadelphia.)

I have just heard that our dear friend, Dr Warren, is no more, but fell gloriously fighting for his country. The constant roar of the cannon is so distressing that we cannot eat, drink or sleep.

E Martin Gay, a Boston Tory, wrote to his brother in Halifax on 8 July 1775:

The famus Doctr Worrin, who had for some year[s] bin a sturer up of Rebelion was kild in the action. [I wish that] some others [like him] which I could name [had] ben there, and meet the same fate with him. It would [have] made the victory of that day the more glorious.

After Dr Warren's death someone stole his expensive clothes and dressed the body in their own old things. Ten months later, when the British troops had left Boston, Warren's friends went looking for the body to give it a hero's burial. Because the clothes had been changed they had great difficulty in finding it. In the end, Paul Revere identified his friend's skull. He had fixed two false teeth for him and recognised his work.

Meanwhile, the Congress in Philadelphia had chosen George Washington to command what became known as the Continental Army. He arrived in Watertown on 2 July and began to organise his troops.

1 a) Look at source A. Find Boston, Bunker Hill and Breeds Hill.
b) Look at source C. Find Boston. Work out where Bunker Hill and Breeds Hill are.
c) Why would the British soldiers in Boston be so anxious to drive the Americans off the hills?

2 Look at source C.
a) Why are there so many small boats on the Charles River?
b) Why do you suppose the British navy set Charlestown on fire?
c) Compare sources A and C. Some people say that the Battle of Bunker Hill is wrongly named. Why do you think this is?

3 Read sources D and E.
a) How did Abigail Adams feel about the death of Joseph Warren?
b) How did Martin Gay feel about it?
c) How can you explain the difference?
d) Name at least one person Martin Gay might be thinking of when he said he wished some others could end up like Dr Warren.

PAST THE POINT OF NO RETURN

Once the Declaration was signed, many things were bound to change.

People tend to think that change is the same as progress. However, this may not always be the case. A historian must make a careful study to find the real effects of change.

1 Work with a neighbour. Think of as many ways as you can in which life in the colonies might change after the Declaration of Independence.

Lots of tales about the signing have been handed down. One story is that John Hancock, President of the Congress, said, 'We must [all agree]. There must be no pulling different ways. We must all hang together.'

'Yes,' Benjamin Franklin is supposed to have replied; 'We must indeed all hang together, or we shall all hang separately.'

And another story says that big Mr Harrison, signing for Virginia, teased little Mr Gerry from Massachusetts that he (Mr Harrison) would be hanged quickly, being so heavy, but little Mr Gerry would be left kicking in the air for half an hour or so.

But even though everyone was nervous it was also very exciting.

A John Adams continued his letter to Abigail on 3 July 1776:

The second day of July, 1776 will be the most memorable [event] in the history of America. It ought to be [celebrated] with parades, games, guns, bells, bonfires and illuminations, from one end of this continent to the other, from this time forward for evermore.

B Fireworks 200 years later, over the Washington Monument, to celebrate the Fourth of July. John Adams was right about everything – except the date!

New countries need a new flag. One of the first new American flags had flown at Bunker Hill. It looked like this.

C The flag flown at Bunker Hill.

There are many stories of how the actual Stars and Stripes flag was born. This is the most popular one:

D George Washington told Betsy Ross about Congress' idea for a new flag, June 1776:
We take the stars from heaven and the red from our Mother country, separating it by white stripes, showing that we have separated from her, and the stripes represent liberty.

Mrs Ross ran an upholstery shop and was a skilled needlewoman. She persuaded him to have five-pointed stars instead of six, because they were easier to cut out. (Try it!) There is no early written evidence that this happened, but Betsy Ross had told the story to her daughters. They passed it on to her grandson.

E Betsy Ross' flag.

Over the next few weeks the Declaration was read in each of the new states. There must have been lots of new flags flying.

F Captain John Paul Jones of the American Navy flew this flag when he captured the British ship *Serapis* off the Yorkshire coast in 1779.

The part of the Declaration you can see in source G has become very famous. If Jefferson had been writing now he might have put it like this: We think these things are obvious. All men are given equal rights by God. No one can take away these rights. Among them are the rights to life, liberty and happiness.

The Gentleman's Magazine, published in London in September 1776, thought the Declaration was silly. The writer said he would not be able to find two men throughout the whole world who were really created equal.

G Part of the Declaration of Independence, 1776:
We hold these truths to be self-evident, that all men are created equal, that they are endowed by their Creator with certain inalienable rights, that among these are life, liberty and the pursuit of happiness.

2 a) Why does the writer of the article in *The Gentleman's Magazine* think the Declaration is silly?
b) What might Jefferson say to explain what he had written?
c) What might one of the slaves on Jefferson's plantation say to him about the Declaration?
d) What might a woman like Abigail Adams say?
e) What does John Adams think about the Declaration?
f) Why do you think John Adams and *The Gentleman's Magazine* writer have such different opinions?

3 a) Why can we be sure of what John Adams exactly said about the Declaration?
b) Are we so sure of the stories about Hancock, Franklin, Harrison and Gerry? Explain your answer.
c) How might a historian set about checking whether or not the stories were true?

4 Work in groups.
a) If you were drawing up a list of important rights for yourselves what would you include?
b) Design a poster to display your ideas.

8 THE WAR OF INDEPENDENCE

1495 1550 1600 1650 1700 1750 1800

A This English drawing made at the time shows the kind of men who were signing on in 1776.

By 1776 it was obvious that there was going to be full-scale war between Britain and her American colonies. They had clashed at Lexington and fought on Bunker Hill. The king had refused to read Congress' petition, and now people were even discussing independence.

The British had problems. They had cut right back on the size of their army. Now they had to find men quickly. Some of the new recruits were of a very low standard.

1 Look at source A. Write down a comment which the inspecting officer might make about each of the three recruits.

The British were forced to bring in mercenaries from Hesse, in Germany. They became known as Hessians. The navy needed strengthening too. Many were press-ganged into action.

After Lexington and Bunker Hill, volunteers flocked to Washington's new army outside Boston. Lord North admitted he knew nothing about military matters, but Britain still felt confident she would soon defeat these amateurs.

However, some of these amateurs were quick learners!

Henry Knox, the bookseller, was now Colonel Knox. He had made an amazing winter journey up to Fort Ticonderoga, near the Canadian border. The fort had been captured from the British, and Washington had asked Knox to bring the big guns down to Boston.

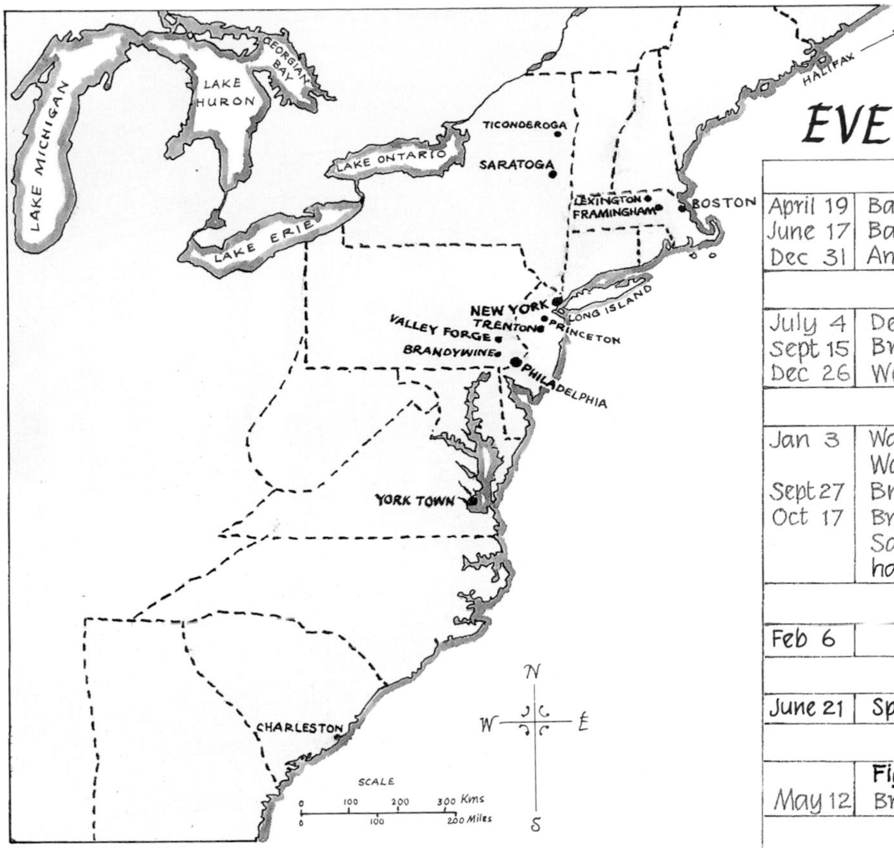
LAKE MICHIGAN
LAKE HURON
GEORGIAN BAY
LAKE ONTARIO
LAKE ERIE
TICONDEROGA
SARATOGA
LEXINGTON
FRAMINGHAM
BOSTON
HALIFAX
NEW YORK
LONG ISLAND
TRENTON
PRINCETON
VALLEY FORGE
BRANDYWINE
PHILADELPHIA
YORK TOWN
CHARLESTON
N
S
E
W
SCALE
0
100
200
300 Kms
0
100
200 Miles

Source B
THE MAIN EVENTS IN THE WAR

1775	
April 19	Battle of Lexington.
June 17	Battle of Bunker Hill.
Dec 31	American attempt to capture Quebec failed.
1776	
July 4	Declaration of Independence.
Sept 15	British captured New York.
Dec 26	Washington won Battle of Trenton
1777	
Jan 3	Washington won Battle of Princeton.
	Washington lost Battle of Brandywine.
Sept 27	British occupied Philadelphia.
Oct 17	British General Burgoyne surrendered at Saratoga. Americans suffered terrible hardships at their Valley Forge winter camp.
1778	
Feb 6	
1779	
June 21	Spanish joined the war.
1780	
	Fighting in the south:
May 12	British win Battle of Charleston.
1781	
Aug 30	French Admiral de Grasse defeated British navy.
Oct 19	Washington won Battle of Yorktown – the final big battle of the war.
1782	
Feb 27	The British House of Commons agreed to end the war
1783	
Sept 3	A Peace Treaty was signed in Paris.

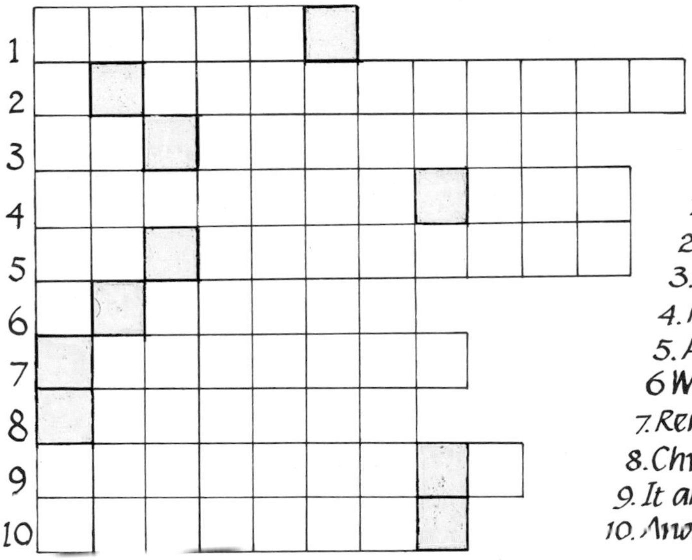
1
2
3
4
5
6
7
8
9
10

CLUES FOR PUZZLE

1. The Americans couldn't capture it.
2. Fell in September, 1777.
3. Turned sour for Washington.
4. Knox brought guns from here.
5. A miserable winter here.
6. Washington nearly got caught near here.
7. Remembering this might give Burgoyne bad dreams.
8. Christmas spirit did not last long here.
9. It all started here.
10. And ended here.

Once the guns were in place on the hills round Boston the British no longer felt safe there. They retreated temporarily to Canada in March 1776.

That was the end of the fighting round Boston. Washington moved his army down to New York. Later in 1776 he was almost captured there.

Most of the fighting over the next two years took place in the Middle Colonies. Then the main action moved down into the Southern Colonies.

B The main events in the war.

2 Copy the puzzle grid above into your exercise book. Then use the clues to fill in the answers. When you have finished, the letters in the shaded squares should spell a place where the British had a victory. Everything you need is in source B or in the text.

WHY DID THE AMERICANS WIN?

A In September 1776, General Howe took New York, shown in this contemporary print.

Historians want to know why things happened as they did, and whether some things had a more important effect than others.

Why did the Americans win? When it was all over, most of them would have said it was because of Washington. But there were many times during the first years of the war when people had doubts about his leadership.

For example, in late 1776, when Howe and Washington were fighting around New York, Howe nearly captured the whole American army. Only the hard work of a regiment of New England fishermen saved it. The fishermen rowed the Americans from Long Island to safety.

In fact, for the first part of the war, Washington seemed much better at organising retreats than at fighting. It was lucky for him that General Howe never bothered to chase him.

Washington had a difficult job. Hardly any of the American army were professional soldiers. Most were craftsmen or farmers. They didn't like army discipline.

But the Americans were fighting in their own land, for their homes and families. They never gave in, and they learned from their mistakes.

B John Adams, years later, asked an old soldier why he had fought. He got this reply:

Young man, what we meant in going for those redcoats was this: we always had governed ourselves, and we always meant to. They didn't mean we should.

American women fought just as hard as the men. Those left at home had twice as much work to do. They ran the farms, they made the ammunition. In any spare time, women like Benjamin Franklin's daughter, Sarah, raised money for food and clothing for the soldiers.

Many women risked their lives with messages. Emily Greiger swallowed hers when stopped by British sentries. She delivered it from memory next day.

Quite a few women became soldiers themselves. Mary McCauley followed her husband into the army. When he was killed in action she took over his cannon and fought on for the rest of the battle. She was one of many women to get a war pension.

Deborah Sampson was another. She pretended she was called Robert Shurtleff, and fought as a soldier. She was wounded and her secret was discovered in hospital. Much later, Paul Revere helped her write letters to get a pension.

1 a) Look at source C. Is the artist proud of Molly Pitcher? Explain how you decided.
b) Here are some feelings which the other soldiers may have had when they found out that Robert Shurtleff was really a woman: anger, amusement, pride, surprise. Try to add more ideas to this list.
c) You are either Deborah Sampson or one of the other soldiers. Write a letter home telling how people felt after it was discovered that Robert was really Deborah.

C This picture shows 'Molly Pitcher'. In May 1788 during the fighting for New York she carried water to the troops and took her wounded husband's place at the guns.

They were fighting a long way from home in a huge, wild country.
SARATOGA 200 miles but don't expect a road
LONDON Over 3000 miles
CHARLESTON 700 miles
NEW YORK
Am I thus protected?
The British Government led by Lord North wasn't well prepared for war.
Some reasons why the British lost
British Generals were inefficient.
Oh dear! Washington has escaped again. Next time we must catch him.
France joined in the war.
At last! Now vee shall 'ave revenge for losing our American lands in 1763

D Some reasons why the British lost.

2 a) Work in groups. Look at source D. Then read pages 44-7 again. List all the reasons you can find which may have helped the Americans win the war.
b) Now choose the three reasons which you think were most important. Explain your choices to the rest of the class.
c) Why is it difficult to make judgements like these?

3 Design a banner or a quilt to celebrate the American victory.

19 PEOPLE TORN IN TWO

1495 1550 1600 1650 1700 1750 1800

A The statue of George III being pulled down by the Sons of Liberty, in July 1776.

When the Declaration of Independence was read in New York, many were delighted, and held a big celebration. They pulled down the statue of George III. The lead was made into musket balls.

Not everyone was pleased. Many New Yorkers, who called themselves Loyalists, still supported the king. The Daughters and Sons of Liberty saw them differently. To them they were Tory traitors.

The war for American Independence was really a civil war, with people of the same country on different sides. Benjamin Franklin's own son, William, was a Loyalist.

Naturally, the Loyalists did not agree with the ideas in Tom Paine's *Common Sense*. They thought they were better off being ruled by the king than by a Congress.

B From *The letters of a Westchester Farmer*, by Samuel Seabury. Written in 1774-5, when Congress was trying to stop imports from Britain of tea, sugar, and wool.

If I must be enslaved, let it be by a KING at least, and not by a parcel of [jumped-up] lawyers. If I must be [eaten], let me be [eaten] by the jaws of a lion, and not gnawed to death by rats . . .

Some Loyalists joined up with Indians to make raids on rebel Americans. One of the cruellest raids was at Cherry Valley in New York State. It was led by a Mohawk Indian called Joseph Brant. Many were scalped . One old lady was tomahawked to death.

British General Clinton strongly condemned these raids. But then a story started to go around about a big sack of women's, children's and babies' scalps. This was supposed to have been delivered to the Canadian Governor to be sent to the 'Great King across the Water'.

In 1777, a young girl, Jane McCrea, had been captured and scalped by Indians fighting with the British General Burgoyne. This had disgusted Americans. Many more men joined Washington's army as a result. Even more joined up after they heard the new story, even though it wasn't true.

C A recruitment drive for the Continental Army (the correct name for the army led by Washington) in the 1770s.

D The murder of Jane McCrea in 1777. Drawn by an artist shortly afterwards.

During war each side tries to persuade people that the other side is in the wrong. They sometimes twist information in order to do this. We call this using propaganda.

Historians argue about just how much ill treatment of Loyalists there was. Certainly some were threatened or badly treated. A Virginian colonel, Charles Lynch, used to lash Loyalists and hang them up by their thumbs.

About 80,000 Loyalists left the country in fear of what might happen. Most went to Canada. Some, like Governor Hutchinson, went to London. He was homesick for America for the rest of his life.

1 Look at source D.
a) What did the artist try to make people feel? Give reasons.
b) Do you think the artist would be successful? Explain your answer.
c) You are a journalist on an American paper owned by one of the Sons of Liberty. Write a report to go with the picture. Try to stir up bad feeling against the British and the Loyalists.

2 The stories about Jane McCrea, and babies' scalps, made good propaganda for American army recruitment. Design a poster, using propaganda ideas, to persuade men to join up to fight the British, Tories and Indians.

3 a) Copy the puzzle grid into your exercise book.
b) Find and ring the words on the right.
c) Write down the one word in the list which is not in the puzzle.
d) The remaining letters, written down in order from the top, reading from left to right, make a battle cry which the rebel Americans used against the Loyalist Indians after 1777. Write it down.

B	A	L	L	R	E	B	E	L
R	E	M	Y	S	B	E	O	A
Y	M	R	N	C	R	Y	B	S
R	E	A	C	A	A	E	T	H
U	R	G	H	L	N	J	A	Y
B	N	U	I	P	T	E	R	M
A	C	S	C	R	W	O	O	L
E	T	R	A	I	T	O	R	E
S	S	E	R	G	N	O	C	A

Congress
Brant
Ball
Rebel
Traitor
Tory
Sugar
Lash
Scalp
Burgoyne
Loyalists
Seabury
Tea
Wool
Lynch

4 a) Make a list of reasons why Loyalists may have wanted to stay as part of the British Empire.
b) Write a letter to relatives back in Britain, saying why you are going to move to Canada or why you have decided to stay. (Perhaps one of your family disagrees – like in the Franklin family.)

20 THIRTEEN STATES OR ONE?

1495 1550 1600 1650 1700 1750 1800

After Yorktown, apart from a few battles here and there, the war was over. It took longer to sign a peace treaty. However, by late 1783 the last British were leaving.

America now had to organise its future. As soon as independence had been declared, the new separate states had begun to draw up Bills of Rights. These said what freedoms their citizens should have.

There was a lot of discussion about whether the 13 new states should unite. People in England were sure they would find it far too difficult. This was because the different states stretched over huge distances, and were separated by high mountain ranges and wide, deep lakes and rivers.

A Should the States unite?

SHOULD THE STATES UNITE?

Some thought NO BECAUSE
1 They wanted to stay independent.
I'm a New Yorker and proud of it.
2 Distances between states were huge and roads were bad.
EXPRESS STAGE COACH
3 They felt there was no need now the war was over.
PEACE! Our troubles are over!
Some thought YES BECAUSE
1 They all spoke the same language.
He may come from Boston, but at least he speaks English
2 They had all fought together in the war.
3 They needed to organise the new lands to the west.
I wish the British army was around to protect us
4 Pirates were attacking American ships.
At least the British navy had its uses
5 They thought it would be better to have just one set of money.
13 sets of coins are too hard to handle

When studying history we often find that new problems force people to change their ideas. The Americans were proud of their separate independent states, but they now faced new problems. Many began to think it might be better to unite.

A Federal Convention was held in 1787. This was a meeting of representatives of all the states except Rhode Island. George Washington was the Convention's President. Its task was to work out a new constitution for the United States. This was a set of rules for governing the states.

It certainly was not an easy job. They all knew some change was necessary, but everyone had different ideas. The first problem was how to stop a government having too much power. They felt they had just got rid of one dictator, so they wanted to be sure they did not get another.

Thomas Jefferson was in Paris, where he had taken over from Franklin as American Minister to France, but he still managed to have a say in planning the constitution. He sent the writings of Polybius and Montesquieu home to his friends.

Polybius was a Greek historian who lived in the second century BC. He thought power should be shared out so that no one had complete power. He thought that the constitution of the Roman Empire was a good example of how this could work. A Frenchman, Montesquieu, writing much later, agreed.

B Montesquieu wrote in his book *The Spirit of the Laws* in 1748:

Constant experience shows us that every man [who has] power is apt to [use it wrongly]. To prevent this it is necessary that power should be a check to power.

When the [lawmaking and ruling] powers are [given] to the same person there can be no liberty. Again there is no liberty, if the [judge's] power is not separated from [lawmaking and ruling].

Some representatives at the Convention wanted to have just one House in their new Congress, elected by all the people. Others thought this would give too much power to the mass of the people. They thought two Houses could check each other. In the end, it was decided to have two Houses, like the British.

The British had the House of Commons and the House of Lords. The Americans called theirs the House of Representatives and the Senate. One big difference was that the American Senate was not hereditary like the House of Lords.

C British Prime Minister, William Pitt, addresses the House of Commons in 1783.

1. Read source B. Copy these sentences into your notebook and choose words from the list to fill the gaps.
   a) Montesquieu thought that people with power often used it ________.
   b) He thought power for lawmaking and power for ruling should be given to ________ people.
   c) He thought this would act as a ________.
   d) He thought that judges should have nothing to do with ________ and ________.
   • ruling • wrongly • different • lawmaking • check
2. Work with a partner. Look at source A.
   a) Write down at least two reasons why people might think the states should not unite.
   b) Now write down at least two problems being faced by Americans at that time.
   c) You are members of your local state parliament, which has been against uniting. Write a speech explaining why you think your state should change its mind and discuss a union.
3. Design a poster to go on display in your state to try to persuade the people that a union of all the states would be a good decision.

21 RIPPLES ROUND THE WORLD

1495	1550	1600	1650	1700	1750	1800

The men who wrote the American constitution would be pleased, but surprised, to find it still in use 200 years later.

They would be even more surprised to find how far round the world their ideas had spread. Sometimes people have a greater influence on things than they expect.

In 1789, just six years after the end of the American Revolution, the French Revolution began. Some of the people you have met in this book were involved in it.

The Marquis de Lafayette, who had fought with Washington, was elected Vice-President of the new French National Assembly. Jefferson was in Paris in 1789, and he helped Lafayette write a Declaration of the Rights of Man. It was passed by the National Assembly in July, 1789.

A In his biography of Jefferson, historian M.D. Peterson described life in Lafayette's home in 1785:

Visitors to his Paris [felt as if they had somehow been moved] to America. [Lafayette] spoke English as readily as French; his children, Virginia and George Washington Lafayette, spoke English and sang American songs, two American Indian boys were part of his household; a copy of the Declaration of Independence hung on the wall of his study in one side of a double frame, the other side empty 'waiting for the Declaration of Rights of France'.

1 Read source A.
a) How do you know that the American Revolution had a big influence on Lafayette?
b) How do you know that he was probably hoping for a French Revolution?
c) Why would Lafayette ask Jefferson to help him write a French Declaration of Rights?

Ideas about freedom were already well-known in Europe. But the Americans had now put the ideas into practice.

France needed change. Many French people wondered if they could learn lessons from America. They liked the idea of no taxation without representation; they liked the idea of the Rights of Man. Some liked the idea of a republic, because they thought the French royal family spent too much of the people's money.

B The Hall Of Mirrors, completed in 1686. One of the magnificent rooms in the Palace of Versailles where the French kings lived.

Many British visitors to France during the 1780s wrote in their diaries that they thought the French were about to have a revolution. They seemed to think there was an American link.

C The Reverend Thomas Pennington wrote in 1782:

The French are [pushing for] their liberty. Having [tried] to obtain it for the Americans, [they] next mean to take care of themselves.

D Arthur Young, a farming journalist visiting France, wrote in 1787:

All ranks of men are eager for some change. A strong [feeling] of liberty [is] increasing every hour since the American revolution.

2 a) Read source C. What does Reverend Pennington mean when he says the French next mean to take care of themselves?
b) Read source D. Does Arthur Young agree with Reverend Pennington? Explain your answer.

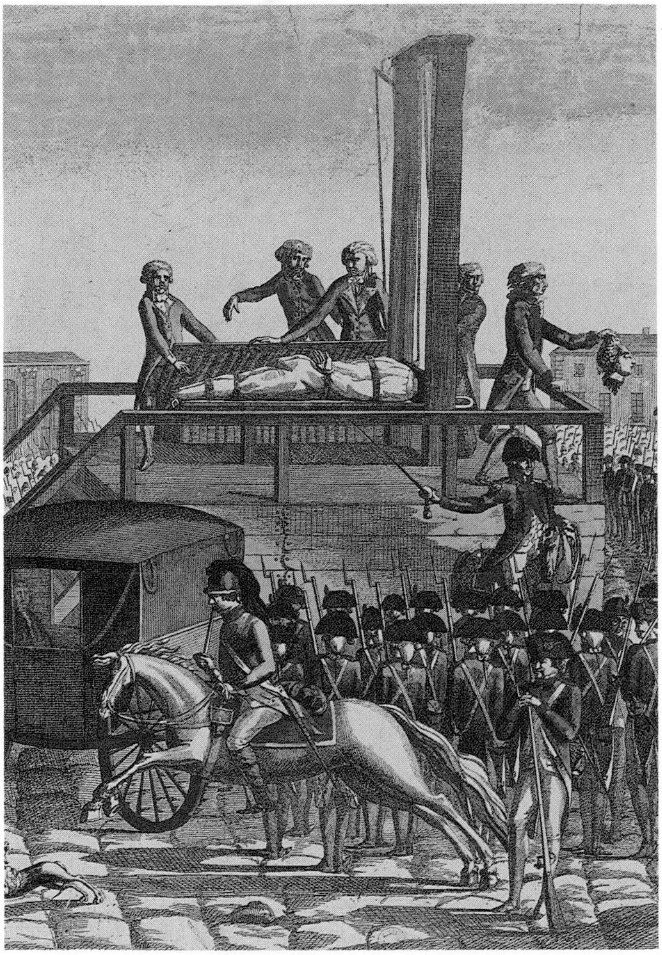

E The execution of the French king, Louis XVI in 1793.

3 Look at source E.
a) What is the man holding up for everyone to see?
b) You are an American. What might you say if a member of the French royal family told you it was America's fault that the king had been killed?

Le Petit Journal
2000000
5

F The Statue of Liberty being built in Paris in 1884. It was to be a gift from the French people to the Americans.

4 Look at source F. Why do you think the French decided to give the Americans this gift?

The ripples caused by the American Revolution didn't just wash up against the shores of Europe.

It was strange to think that Spain had helped the 13 colonies in their war for independence, because the Spanish had colonies of their own in South and Central America. The colonists of this Spanish empire were able to watch 13 New World colonies shake off the rule of the British king. By 1824 they had done the same thing themselves and won independence from Spain.

This seems really easy. Perhaps we should try it on the King of Spain, amigos.
TONIGHT'S CONTEST
GEORGE III
V
YANKEE DOODLE DANDY

22 AND THEN?

So what came next? Benjamin Franklin died in 1790, but he lived long enough to see the first President sworn in.

John Hancock, the first man to sign the Declaration of Independence, lived until 1793. Hancock was rather vain. He would have been very proud of his funeral procession – the best New England had ever seen.

1 Using the index to find information, write an obituary for either Franklin, Revere, Hewes or Washington.

George Washington was persuaded to serve a second term of four years as President. He finally got back to his farm at Mount Vernon in 1797, and he died there in late 1799.

Paul Revere ended up with a fortune from bellmaking and copper production. Rachel died in 1813 and Paul in 1818. He died on a Sunday, when bells he had made would have been ringing all over the States.

Mr Harrison and Mr Gerry were not hanged. Each survived to old age, in spite of having signed the Declaration of Independence.

Thomas Jefferson and John Adams went on to become Presidents of the United States. Both died on the fiftieth anniversary of the Declaration of Independence – 4 July 1826. Adams was 91. Abigail had died eight years earlier.

Old George Hewes beat them all. He continued to tell his tales of the Boston Tea Party right up till his death in 1840. We are not certain how old he was. His family claim he was 109!

What of the country itself? In the 19th century many settlers moved into the western plains following the new railroad. The buffalo which had lived there were wiped out. The Plains Indians fought bravely for the right to live the way they always had, but they were doomed.

A A buffalo hunt. Indians used the hide for clothes and wigwams, the meat for food, the bones for tools and the droppings for fuel.

B When the Indians found that arrows and rifles were no use they tried to derail the trains, as shown in this 1867 painting.

C In 1877, Chief Joseph of the Nez Perces tribe gave up the struggle. This was his speech of surrender:

Our chiefs are killed. The little children are freezing to death. My people have no blankets, no food.

Hear me, my chiefs; I am tired; my heart is sick and sad. From where the sun now stands, I will fight no more forever.

2 Read source C and look at sources A and B.
a) What might well-meaning friends suggest that Chief Joseph and his tribe should do to mend their lives?
b) Why will it be hard for them to take any advice?
c) Why would the Indians find it hard to hold back the progress of the railroad?

How did the new country treat its women? Most of the Daughters of Liberty had run the family businesses and often defended the homes, while their husbands became soldiers or politicians. Even so, they had to wait until 1920 before they were allowed to vote in US Federal Elections.

Slaves had to wait even longer. They were officially freed in 1863, but black people did not have real freedom until much later.

One thing certainly stayed the same. Immigrants from Europe kept on sailing to America to start a new life, just as the first colonists had done.

D From a poem by Emma Lazarus about the Statue of Liberty.

Give me your tired, your poor, your huddled masses
yearning to breathe free.

E 'In the Land of Promise': a painting from 1884 showing immigrants who have just arrived in New York.

3 Look at source E and read source D.
a) Make a list of questions for a partner to answer about the picture so that they get as much information as possible from it.
b) Do you think the painter of the picture in source E may have read Emma Lazarus' poem? Explain your answer.

4 Study the credits for any American television programme. Nearly all Americans are descended from immigrants. See if you can work out where some of the people involved in the television programme have their roots.

23 ALL MEN ARE CREATED EQUAL?

Thomas Paine was not the only Briton who was pleased about the American Revolution. There were quite a few. They were known as Radicals . Many of them belonged to societies which met in the evenings to discuss how Britain might be changed.

A James Boswell wrote in his diary for 21 September 1769, about a club which met at St Paul's Coffee House in London:

We have wine and punch upon the table. Some of us smoke a pipe, conversation goes on. At nine there is a sideboard with [toasted cheese] and Apple Puffs, and Beer. [It costs about 7½p per head.]

Much was said this night against the Parliament. I said that, as it seemed to be agreed that all members of Parliament became [bad] it was better to choose men already bad, and so save good men.

Benjamin Franklin often visited this club. Another member was Dr Richard Price, a Welsh preacher who wrote a book called *Observation on the Nature of Civil Liberty*. He wrote it the same year that the American Declaration of Independence was signed. The ideas in his book agreed with the Declaration. The Americans were so pleased that they made him an honorary citizen.

The Radicals wanted changes in the British parliamentary system, and they wanted more men to have a vote. They found the changes in America very encouraging.

B John Cartwright wrote a book in 1777 in favour of changing the parliamentary system. (This extract from it has been made simpler.)

Parliament is in a mess. We should have elections every year, not every seven years. It is wrong that Parliament should treat this suggestion as a big joke. At the moment 214,000 people vote to send 513 MPs to Parliament. These MPs are supposed to represent 6 million people. *And* 254 of these MPs are elected by only 5,723 people. These people pretend they have a right to do this. But it is completely unjust.

It was actually worse than this, because he had not counted all the women in Britain. They were going to have to wait even longer for a vote.

People in France also wanted changes. This led to the French Revolution, as we saw in Chapter 21. The French took away the power of the Catholic Church and the power of the nobles . They killed the king and queen. This led to war with most European countries. Real peace did not return until 1815.

Times were bad in Britain in 1819. Many people were unemployed and food was expensive after bad harvests. The Government worried that there might be a British Revolution, bringing really big changes like there had been in France.

So when the Radicals organised a peaceful meeting at St Peter's Fields in Manchester in 1819 it was broken up by the local part-time soldiers. Eleven people were killed, and 560 wounded. This event became known as Peterloo, because the Radicals said the violence was as bad as the Battle of Waterloo, which had been fought against the French just four years earlier.

C The Battle of Peterloo, August 1819. On top of the banners on the platform you can see 'caps of liberty' like people wore in the French Revolution.

Another group of people welcomed the American Revolution. They hoped it might make it easier to get rid of slavery. This group, led by a man called Granville Sharp, had already managed to get a judge to rule that slavery was illegal inside Britain. But they wanted to stop the buying and selling of slaves everywhere, and then to end slavery altogether.

D Granville Sharp was told some horrifying stories. He wrote in his diary in March 1783:

Gustavus Vassa, a negro, called on me with an account of 130 Negroes being thrown alive into the sea from on board an English slave ship.

The slaves had been on board the *Zong*, and were drowned because the ship was running short of water. When the case was heard in court the judge said that although it was very shocking it was 'the same as if horses had been thrown overboard'.

E This early 19th-century picture was drawn for an anti-slavery leaflet. It shows a 15-year-old slave girl being punished because she would not sleep with the sailors.

People against slavery in America and Britain joined together to fight it, but their job got harder after American Independence. This was because the British West Indian colonies seemed more important once the American colonies had been lost. Slaves did most of the hard work there, and many West Indian landowners were members of the British parliament.

In spite of this, people like Sharp, Thomas Clarkson and William Wilberforce continued to fight against slavery. In 1807, trading in slaves by British people was banned. In 1833 a law was passed to start freeing all British-owned slaves.

1 Read source A. Do you think Boswell really means that only bad people should be in Parliament? Explain your answer.

2 Look at source C.
a) What sorts of people can you see at the meeting?
b) Why do you think they were treated so fiercely?

3 Look at source E.
a) Write down those things that tell you the picture is drawn by someone who thinks that what is happening is wrong.
b) Can you be sure that what is shown is accurate? Explain your answer.

4 Work in small groups.
Either (a) Plan a leaflet, with illustrations, to be used as anti-slavery propaganda.
Or (b) Write a letter to *The Times* newspaper in 1819, saying why you think it was right to break up the St Peter's Fields meeting with armed soldiers.

24 A NEW EMPIRE

John Adams, the American politician, expected a British revolution to follow the American one. It did not happen.

Although losing the colonies was a terrible blow at first, the British soon pulled themselves together. The loss did not have the bad effects that people feared. In fact, by the 1790s the new United States was buying twice as much from Britain as the old American colonies had done 30 years earlier.

Britain still had Canada. Many Loyalists from the old colonies were given enough compensation money to buy land there.

Britain also had important trading posts in India. She now concentrated on building up these. Lord Cornwallis, who had lost the Battle of Yorktown, became the Governor-General of India in 1784.

For the next 153 years Britain controlled India. Huge profits were made from things like silks, salt, jewels, the drug opium, cotton and tea.

B India had a big effect on the English language as well. Here are a few of the words from India which have become part of English:
jungle, curry, cot, polo, verandah, punch, bangle, loot, dinghy, juggernaut, thug, jute.

However, the British did have one problem after the American colonies became independent. In the past many people found guilty of theft or fighting had been transported to America. There they were sold like slaves to work in the plantations. Skilled men sold for £15-20, women for £8-10.

This trade stopped after American Independence. Britain needed a new place where convicts could be sent. Very quickly things became desperate. The prisons were overflowing, and many prisoners were being held on big old ships called hulks on the River Thames, and at Portsmouth.

Joseph Banks, who had sailed to Australia and New Zealand with the explorer, Captain Cook, ten years earlier, suggested that Australia would be a good place to send convicts. In May 1787, the first shiploads set sail for Botany Bay, New South Wales. There were 750 convicts on board, and 200 Marines. They arrived in January 1788. Over the next 50 years many more followed.

A A British wife in India 200 years ago supervises her servants.

C Here are some of the people sentenced at a court in Gloucester in 1826:

Wm. Williams, for attempting to commit a rape on Hannah Roberts, an infant 10 years of age. – 3 Years Imp[risonment].

Wm. George, Thos. Parker, and Eliza Parker for housebreaking at Old Sodbury, and stealing a bedquilt. – 7 Years Transp.[ortation].

George Cooke, for housebreaking at Dursley, and stealing a tea caddy and other articles. – 7 Years Transp.

Wm. Chivers, for breaking open the house of Francis Cam and stealing 21 cheeses. – Transp. for Life.

Isaiah John Langstreeth, for stealing tea, at Tewkesbury. – 7 Years Transp.

George Goode, for killing T. Hawkins at St. Briavels. – 18 months Imp.

D Lieutenant Clark of the Marines sailed with the first convict ships. Here are excerpts from his diary for May and June 1787:

Flog this day John Bennet, a convict, with 87 lashes for breaking out of irons.

Capt. Meredith put the four convict women, Elizabeth Dudgeon, Margaret Hall, Elizabeth Pully, Charlotte Ware out of irons, whom I had put in irons for fighting. They are a disgrace to their whole sex, that they are. I wish all of the women were out of the ship.

1 Look at source A.
a) How many servants has the woman?
b) What are they all doing?
c) List the ways in which this woman's life was good.
d) How may she have found her life difficult?

2 Look at source C. Work with a partner.
a) Put the crimes into order, with the ones you think are worst first.
b) Compare your list with the punishments the judge gave at Gloucester. Is it the same or different? Try to work out reasons for any differences.
c) Which of the people would be punished more severely today? Give reasons.
d) Which of the people would be punished less severely? Again, give reasons.
e) What does this tell you about how attitudes have changed? Explain your answer in detail.

E The Royal Pavilion, Brighton. It was built as the Prince Regent's seaside house. It was created for him by various architects between 1787 and 1822.

25 CHANGE AND CONTINUITY

Lord North was forced to resign. He had been Prime Minister for 12 years so that was a big change in British politics.

At first, Britain and the United States got on badly after American independence. They even had another short war in 1812. But eventually they forgave each other. After all, they did speak the same language, and a great many Americans had their roots in Britain.

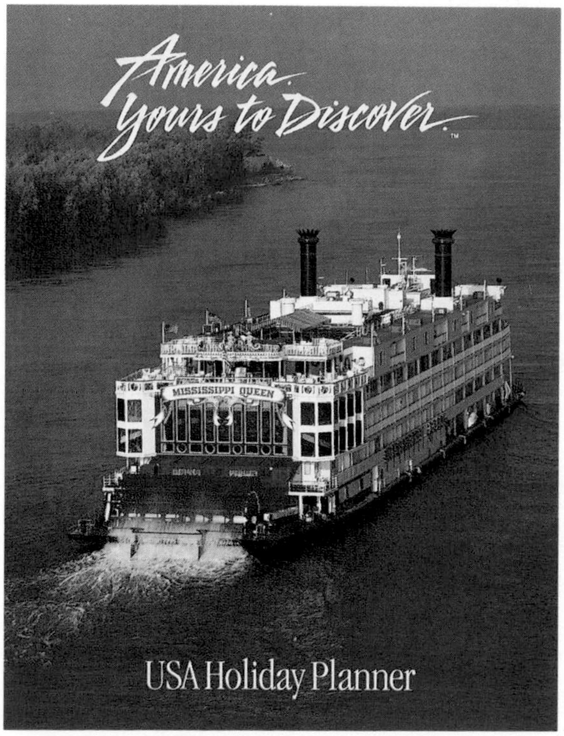

America
Yours to Discover
MISSISSIPPI QUEEN
USA Holiday Planner

A The United States is now a favourite holiday destination for British people.

If you arrive in Boston by plane now you can take a waterbus from the airport across the harbour and land at Rowe's Wharf. John Rowe, the diary-keeping merchant, would probably not recognise it. There is a modern luxury hotel built on it.

Griffin's Wharf, where George Hewes, Thomas Melvill and the rest tipped the tea into the harbour, has gone. But there is a copy of one of the teaships anchored nearby. You can visit it and hurl teachests overboard!

Rachel and Paul Revere would find their house, and Paul's mother's house, still standing. John Hancock would be very proud to see the skyscraper pictured in source B.

B The 890 feet high John Hancock Mutual Life Insurance Tower.

The United States still uses the Federal Constitution drawn up in 1787. But now the states stretch from the Atlantic to the Pacific. Nobody expected that in 1787.

C Modern New York.

In the earlier part of this century Americans began to worry that too many of their old buildings were being destroyed to make way for modern ones.

In 1926, John D. Rockefeller, an American multi-millionaire, agreed to give money to preserve Williamsburg, the old capital of Virginia.

Williamsburg is now a living museum. All the old colonial buildings have been restored. If you look at sources B and C on page 6 you can see the Virginia Parliament House in Williamsburg. If Jefferson or Washington could stroll through the streets they would feel quite at home.

Washington would even be able to visit his favourite inn, Christina Campbell's Tavern. Craftspeople are at work in all the shops, binding books, making wigs, printing newspapers.

D Young musicians play colonial music on fifes and drums at Williamsburg.

In Lancaster County, Pennsylvania, there is a group of people called the Amish. They are descended from Germans who arrived in 1737, looking for religious freedom. They will not have mains electricity and they have horse-drawn carriages instead of cars. They still speak a kind of German.

The men always wear special wide-brimmed hats outside the house, while the women wear aprons and bonnets. They have their own schools.

But they do ride in taxis, use battery electricity in their dairies, and have telephones in sheds at the end of their lanes. And they play baseball and eat hamburgers barbecued on gas grills.

During the 1980s a film called 'Witness', starring Harrison Ford and Kelly McGillis, was made. It was supposed to be set in an Amish community. The Amish were very angry, because they disapprove of films. They threatened to leave Pennsylvania and search once again for religious freedom.

The state of Pennsylvania has always given religious freedom to all its citizens. State officials held talks with the Amish to try to make sure that they were not upset again.

1 Look at source C. Then look at source A on page 46 which shows New York in 1776. Make a list of all the differences you can find between the two pictures.

2 If you asked Mr Rockefeller why he had given money to restore Williamsburg, what do you think he might say?

3 a) Why do you think the Amish disapprove of things like cars, television and electricity?
b) Why do you think they allow battery electricity, taxi-riding, etc.?
c) Make two lists: (i) a list of ways in which the lives of the Amish have stayed the same over the the past 250 years, and (ii) a list of ways in which their lives have changed.

GLOSSARY

ballads – simple songs
bloody backs – slang name for British soldiers, partly because of their red coats, and partly because they were whipped a lot as punishment
chamber pots – pots to hold urine, usually kept under the bed
charters – letters from a king or queen giving certain rights
compensation – money paid to make up for a loss
culprit – guilty person, wrongdoer
dame school – first or primary school, usually kept by an elderly lady, in her own home
dictator – someone who rules a country with total power
disembowelled – when the bowels and stomach have been ripped out
elegantly – with style
elementary school – first or primary school
endowed – given, born with
Governor-general – person appointed by a king or queen to run a colony for them
hatches – openings in a ship's deck, leading to the cargo below
heirloom – something precious passed down in a family from parent to son or daughter
hereditary – passed down from parent to son or daughter
honorary – given as an honour
inalienable – cannot be taken away
indentured – bound by an agreement to work for a master
irons – chains or bands of iron
legal – to do with the law
lottery – raffle with money as prizes
Marines – soldiers on a warship
mercenaries – professional soldiers, paid to fight for another country
midwives – people who deliver babies
mobbish – noisy, badly behaved
mother country– the country from which most of the colonists came (Britain)
moulting – losing old fur ready for a new growth
negro – black person
nobles – lords and ladies
parley – talk to settle points of disagreement
petition – letter, signed by many people, asking the king for help
pewter – mugs or plates made from a mixture of tin and lead
plains – level flat country west of the 13 colonies
plantation – country estate which farms tobacco, cotton, etc
press-ganged – forced to serve in the army or navy
radicals – people who want to make big changes
ratify – agree to
repeal – withdraw (a law)
representative – person chosen to give the views of other people in a Parliament or similar organisation
republic – country in which the head of state is chosen by the people or their elected representatives
Rope-walk – workshop where rope was made
scalped – had the skin and hair taken from the top of the head as a victory prize
sermon – religious talk, often given as part of a church service
swearing-in-ceremony – special meeting where Washington made promises and became President
traitors – people who betray their rulers or their countries
transported – sent to another country as a punishment
yearning – longing